ANCESTOR WORSHIP AND CHRISTIANITY IN KOREA

ANCESTOR WORSHIP AND CHRISTIANITY IN KOREA

Jung Young Lee
Editor

Studies in Asian Thought and Religion
Volume 8

The Edwin Mellen Press
Lewiston●Queenston
Lampeter

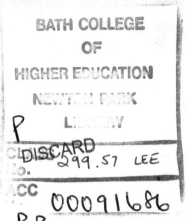
Library of Congress Cataloging-in-Publication Data

Ancestor worship and Christianity in Korea / Jung Young Lee, editor.
    p. cm. -- (Studies in Asian thought and religion ; v. 8)
    ISBN 0-88946-059-0
    1. Ancestor worship--Korea. 2. Christianity--Korea. 3. Korea-
-Religion. I. Lee, Jung Young. II. Series.
    [BL467.A49 1989]
    299'.57--dc19   88-39988
                                                                              CIP

This is volume 8 in the continuing series
Studies in Asian Thought & Religion
Volume 8 ISBN 0-88946-059-0
SATR Series ISBN 0-88946-050-7

The Edwin Mellen Press

Box 450   Box 67
Lewiston, New York   Queenston, Ontario
14092 USA   L0S 1L0 CANADA
Mellen House
Lampeter, Dyfed, Wales
UNITED KINGDOM SA48 7DY

Printed in the United States of America

To My People
in the Land of Morning Calm

Contents

Contributors

Young-cahn Ro is Associate Professor of Religious Studies at George Mason University in Fairfax, Virginia.

Myung Hyuk Kim is Professor of Historical Theology at Hapdong Presbyterian Theological Seminary in Seoul.

Ki-bok Ch'oe is a Catholic priest who has completed his doctorate on Confucianism at Sun Kyun Kwan University in Seoul.

Pyun Young Tai was a prominent Christian leader during the Japanese colonial period.

Bong-ho Son is Professor at the Asian Center for Theological Studies and Mission in Seoul.

Wi Jo Kang is Professor of Missions at Wartburg Theological Seminary in Dubuque, Iowa.

Jung Young Lee is Professor and Chairperson of Religious Studies at the University of North Dakota in Grand Forks, North Dakota.

ANCESTOR WORSHIP AND CHRISTIANITY IN KOREA

Introduction

Since the early days of the Christian missions in Asia, ancestor worship has been the focus of many controversies. Korea, having been dominated for five hundred years by the Confucian rule of the Yi dynasty, regarded ancestor worship as a most important national ritual. Thus, everyone in those days, regardless of his religious preference, was expected to participate in the practice. When Christianity was first introduced into Korea about two hundred years ago through Korean emissaries to China, Chinese Christians had already been prohibited from practicing ancestor worship. The activities of early Christian missions in Korea had suffered severely because of the inability of Christianity to accommodate ancestor worship. During the period of Japanese control, Korean Christians had to confront the problem of Shinto worship, which had been understood as the crystallization of Japanese ancestor worship. Korean Christians were, in fact, forced to participate in the Shinto worship. One of the important results achieved during this period was the compromise made by the Roman Catholic Church, which accommodated, with some alteration, the practice of ancestor worship, viewing it as a form of civil ceremony. Most Protestant Christians in Korea believed, however, that the practice of ancestor worship was incompatible with the Christian faith. Most Protestants still strongly resist the practice while failing to find a real solution to the problem.

This volume therefore, addresses the many Protestant Christians who have not found a solution to the problem of how to deal with ancestor worship, a perplexity which has posed a great hindrance to the witness and mission of Christian life in Korea. This volume also addresses many Christians in the Third World, where the practice of ancestor worship is a part of their cultural phenomena. "Can a Christian conscientiously participate in the practice of ancestor worship?" This is the question that I hope to address here. With Christianity expanding so rapidly as to become one of the most powerful forces in Korea, the Christians of Korea are almost compelled to resolve and answer the question of ancestor worship, which is still fundamental to the religious, ethical, and cultural life of the Korean people.

In dealing with the problem of ancestor worship, it is essential first to clarify the meaning and significance of ancestor worship within the Korean context. The first chapter of this volume, therefore, deals with its nature and significance from the perspective of Korean tradition.[1] When first presented (in 1983), this paper made an important contribution to a methodological issue. Arguing that the idea of worship is relative to the various cultural and traditional contexts in which it appears, this chapter helps us weigh the importance of context in the definition and understanding of ancestor worship.

The second chapter attempts to grant the practice of ancestor worship its appropriate place within the history of the Korean churches, particularly of the Protestant tradition in Korea. Thus, it presents an excellent summary of the historical development in the conflict between Christianity and ancestor worship in Korea. It depicts succinctly the problems that Christianity has confronted with respect to ancestor worship from the early days to the present while working among the Korean people. It also helps us also understand the various critical issues and problems that many Korean Protestant leaders have had to deal with in regard to the practice of ancestor worship.[2]

Inasmuch as ancestor worship was officially cannonized by Confucianism and became the core of Confucian ethical practice, it is important to understand the Confucian notion of ancestor worship. Therefore, the third chapter provides a comprehensive treatise on the practice from the perspective of Confucian philosophy written by a Roman Catholic priest, who reflects also the position of Catholicism on the issue of ancestor worship. Since Catholicism has accommodated the practice, this chapter may serve as a guideline for many Protestant Christian leaders in Korea in their efforts to deal with the problem of such worship.[3]

The fourth chapter is an early attempt to explain to western missionaries during the Japanese occupation of Korea why ancestor worship in Korea is not a form of idol worship. This is important because it is an effort by an early Christian to justify and accommodate the practice of ancestor worship in Korea. Although it lacks, eloquence, it elucidates the main issue of ancestor worship and provides an avenue for the possible indignation of Christianity in Korea.[4]

As one of the potential solutions to the problem of ancestor worship, the fifth chapter presents the fascinating thesis that the traditional practice of ancestor worship has been gradually losing its significance in the modern world. It is an attempt to suggest that the practice of ancestor worship in Korea may no longer be a live issue in the Christian mission and witness. This argument is based upon personal observations of the lives of the Korean people as reflecting a deterioration of Confucian influence through the growing secularization of society and the strong impact of Christian influence. If this thesis were correct, the practice of ancestor worship would no longer be an issue for Christianity; to conclude that it is the case, however, may be too simplistic.[5]

The sixth chapter attempts to go beyond a mere accommodation to ancestor worship as being a part of the cultural and civic life of the Korean people. Viewing such worship positively, it suggests that the existing form of ancestor worship can be used as a means of Christian Eucharist to reform Christian family life in Korea. This suggestion is a bold one; and it may create some controversy among Korean Christians. A careful theological study is, in fact, needed before attempting to reform the sacrament of the Lord's Supper.[6]

In the final chapter, I have attempted to provide some guidelines to follow in dealing with the problem of ancestor worship in Korea. After analyzing the various critical problems that ancestor worship poses to the Christian faith, I have concluded that the primary issue is theological. Therefore, this concluding chapter provides a theological perspective in terms of which ancestor worship can be creatively accommodated within the context of Korean Christianity.

Notes

[1]This essay was originally presented to the Consultation on Korean Religions at the 1983 annual meeting of the American Academy of Religion in Dallas. I had the privilege of chairing the Consultation and evaluating the essay.

[2]This essay was formally presented to the Consultation on Christian Response to Ancestor Practice, December, 1983, in Taipei. I consider it a privilege to include the essay in this volume.

[3]The original essay was entitled "The Abolition of Ancestral Rites and Tablets by Catholicism in the Chosen Dynasty and the Basic Meaning of Confucian Ancestral Rites." It appeared in the KOREA JOURNAL. Only the last portion of the essay is included here.

[4]The material comprising this chapter is extracted from a book entitled MY ATTITUDE TO ANCESTOR WORSHIP, Published by the Christian Literature Society of Korea, Seoul, 1926.

[5]This paper was originally written for the Consultation on Christian Response to Ancestor Practices, held in December, 1983, in Taipei. I am grateful to include it in this work.

[6]This essay was originally presented to the Consultation on Korean Religions at the 1983 annual meeting of the American Academy of Religion in Dallas.

Chapter 1

Ancestor Worship: From the Perspective of Korean Tradition

Young-chan Ro

1. The idea of worship and Korean religiosity

Ancestor worship is, indeed, a form of worship. In order to understand the nature of ancestor worship, we must first examine the concept of "worship" in general. Although it is not my intention to explore the nature and function of worship in an exhaustive manner, I shall nonetheless make a preliminary attempt here to clarify the notion of worship. To be sure, the term "ancestor worship" may not be the most accurate translation of "che-sa" (祭祀). .Some have suggested "ancestor cult" instead of "ancestor worship." I do not find, however, that "ancestor cult" is a better or more accurate translation than "ancestor worship"; rather, "ancestor cult" may create an unnecessary confusion because of the pejorative connotations of the term "cult." Hence, I have no intention of introducing another term. "Ancestor ceremony" or "ancestor ritual" are also used; but these terms do not reveal that deeper religious significance that is involved in ancestor worship. Worship is more than a ritual or a ceremony. The idea of worship reflects, as the others do not, various forms of human religiosity.[1] Many religious traditions have formulated and developed their own unique forms of worship. And different forms reflect different ideas of worship. Or we may say, conversely, that different ideas of worship create different forms of worship.

Since worship is one of the most concrete forms of human religiosity, one of the most effective ways of understanding a particular people's religiosity or spirituality is to investigate its forms of worship. The investigation of various forms of worship requires, however, a proper method. Yet a method that is employed in the investigation of one form of worship may not be proper for investigating another form. Moreover, a definition of worship that is formulated in one religious tradition may not be applicable to another tradition. The very notion of worship may differ from one tradition to another. The Judeo-Christian idea of worship, for example, should not be applied to the study of ancestor worship, despite the fact that it is a form of worship. One of the most serious mistakes that Western Christian missionaries have made with respect to ancestor worship was to impose the Christian concept of worship upon the study of ancestor worship, which was formulated within an entirely different religious context and spiritual atmosphere from that of Christian worship.

Ancestor worship viewed as a specific form of worship, needs a proper method or investigation. Ancestor worship not only manifests the religious consciousness and spirituality of the people who practice it, but also reflects their world view, life style, and value system. In this sense, the study of ancestor worship should reflect a comprehensive understanding of the people who created, developed, and preserved such worship. Worship is a comprehensive way of experiencing and a concrete form of expressing man's relationship to gods, spirits, the universe, nature, society, family, and man himself. Ancestor worship may be fruitless without an understanding of the particular Weltanschauung of that specific form of worship. We may even destroy the very nature of ancestor worship if we analyze it with a distinctively Western Christian conceptual tool. I do not, however, intend to deny or reject the validity of a universal phenomenon of worship appearing in the various cultures of the world. What I am trying to point out is that a particular form of worship must not be allowed to lose its unique significance by absorption into a general form of conceptualization. If we wish to understand the meaning of ancestor worship, we have to understand first that idea of worship which is peculiar to the phenomenon of ancestor worship. Different forms of worship are not just so many different forms of expressing the same religiosity or spirituality. Both the form of worship and the idea of it are intrinsically related to each other. Our task, in this regard, is twofold: 1) to examine the idea of worship in the Korean religious context, and 2) to investigate the intrinsic relationship between the Korean native or traditional idea of worship and the development of ancestor worship.

2. The nature of native Korean worship

The ancient Koreans had certain well-established forms of worship. The prototype of worship in Korea is found in the following ancient rituals: Tong-maeng (東盟) in Koguryo (高句麗), Yong-go (迎鼓) in Puyo (扶餘), Mu-chun (舞天) in Ye (濊), and So-do (蘇塗) in Han (韓).[2] These forms of worship were performed usually in the fall along with the celebration of the harvest. The common characteristics of these ancient worships were as follows: 1) The prayer of petition for rich blessings and a good fortune in the coming year. 2) The expression of gratitude to heaven for the blessings to come in the next year. 3) Interaction with the divine spirit. 4) A communal festival accompanied by eating, drinking, music and dancing.[3]

The ancient Koreans did not distinguish between the realms of the sacred and the secular. The forms of worship were both deeply religious and secular at the same time. The most serious religious ritual was likewise the most joyous: the occasion of the celebration of life and the festival of the harvest. The sacred ceremony and the secular festival were harmoniously combined in these forms of worship. The goal of worship was not the salvation of "the soul" or "eternal life," but rather the enrichment of life in this world. Moreover, the object of worship was not clearly defined in terms of a particular deity. The most comprehensive and well-known deity was a personified deity in heaven who was called Han-ul nim. The ancient Korean form of worship was much more concerned about material blessings and a comfortable life than about any life after death. Thus worship was not considered as a ritual separated from daily activities, but rather as a ritual expression of this life's total concerns. In this regard, worship for the ancient Koreans was not exclusively a "sacred" activity. The Korean form of worship did not intend to focus on one single object. Rather the objects of worship varied depending on the occasion of worship; and sometimes a multiplicity of "gods" and "spirits" were worshiped at the same time. Thus, the Korean form of worship was not exclusively related or oriented to a monotheistic God. In other words, the Korean form of worship was an inclusive rather than an exclusive type.[4]

3. The development of ancestor worship in Korea

The origin of ancestor worship in Korea can be traced back to the period of the Three-Kingdoms. Ancestor worship during the Three-Kingdoms era was limited mainly to the royal families.[5] Pack-che (百 濟) had a form of ancestor worship for venerating the founding father, On-cho (溫 祖). Silla (新 羅) and Koguryo (高 句 麗) had a similar form for venerating their own founding fathers. These worships were conducted four times a year following the change of seasons. The definitive form of ancestor worship, however, was not established until the end of the Koryo (高麗) dynasty and the beginning of the Yi dynasty (15th century), when Korean Neo-Confucian scholars such as Paek Yi-chung (白 頤 正) and Chong Mong-Ju (鄭 夢 周) introduced the Han and T'ang systems of ancestor worship into Korea. The popularization of ancestor worship among Korean families, including the establishment of a family-lineage shrine in each individual household, was largely due to the official recognition of Confucianism as the ruling ideology for the Yi dynasty. Although Buddhism was the most dominant religion during the periods of the Three-Kingdoms and the Koryo dynasty, ancestor worship, including the three-year mourning ritual, was still practiced. This continuance shows that the Confucian influence, along with ancestor worship, was still strong in the Three-Kingdoms and Koryo societies even when Buddhism was the dominant religion.

The development of the Korean-form of ancestor worship occurred through the process of combining the traditional or native Korean form of worship with the Chinese form of Confucian ancestor worship. The earlier native forms of worship that appeared in Yong-go, Tong-maeng, Mu-chun, and So-do had continuously influenced the later forms of ritual and worship, including ancestor worship. When Buddhism was the predominant religion in Korea (Silla and Koryo), the most popular rituals, both sacred and secular, were Pal-Kwan hoe (八 關 會) and Yon-dung hoe (燃 燈 會). Despite their formal relationship with Buddhism, these rituals reflected the Korean native religiosity and indigenous forms of worship.[6] In other words, the spirit of the native or indigenous ideas and forms of worship was transmitted by way of the forms of popular Buddhist ritual. The idea of the "celebration" of life and the significance of man's relationship to the "spirits" and "gods" with respect to material blessings were well presented in these Buddhist rituals. The participants in these celebrations and acts of worship were not exclusively concerned with "sacred" objects, but extended their devotions to "secular" objects as well. The focal point of these rituals was the well-being of the community or, sometimes, that of the entire state and nation. These rituals entailed a certain shamanistic belief system: that they were the means for preventing calamities and involving god's blessings, and for protecting the nation with the help of the departed spirits.[7]

Shamanism, as the oldest form of religious belief in Korea, has always been the most influential religious tradition. Due to its flexibility and receptivity, shamanism has been successfully incorporated into other major religious traditions, such as those of Buddhism, Taoism, Confucianism, and Christianity that have been introduced to Korea. The nature of shamanistic spirituality is to seek a resolution for the conflicts caused by physical and social disorders or cosmic disharmony. These conflicts often appeared in a form of disease, a loss of life, immature death, calamities by unknown reasons, etc. These conflicts, however, according to the shamanistic spirituality, can be resolved by a shaman who is supposed to possess the power of relating the world of man to the world of the "spirit" and "gods," the living to the dead. In doing so, a shaman is able to go beyond the boundaries of the duality and to make a harmonious relationship between the conflicting two worlds. Thus, a shaman is able to communicate with the dead, the sick, appease the malice of evil spirits, and invoke the protection of the benevolent ones. Shamanism in Korea goes as far back as Tangun, a mystic figure who is supposed to be the founder of the ancient Choson.[7] Tangun, as the descendent of heaven, was a shaman-king who symbolized the relationship between the heaven and earth.[8] The common characteristics of Korean shamanism maintain a non-dualistic world view. The basic structure of the Tangun myth (檀君 神話), which reflects the original form of Korean shamanism, is based on the non-duality of man and gods (or spirits), life and death, the sacred and the secular, etc. The shamanism transcending any form of duality in time and space represented a common trend in the native Korean folk traditions. The experience of ecstasy was common among those who participated in the shamanistic ritual; and in this ecstasy, man could find release from his own self-consciousness and was able to engage in a dialogue with "gods" and "spirits."

The non-dualistic nature of Korean shamanism has led to a uniquely Korean form of worship, involving the non-duality of the sacred and the secular, of religious ritual and secular play, of men and gods, and of spiritual and material life. This non-dualistic feature should not be understood, however, as a monistic tendency. In monism, there is no distinction whatever, for example, between gods and men, spirit and matter, good and evil. Non-dualism, however, does still recognize the distinctions between the two seemingly opposing aspects in each of these pairs, while it does not separate them as two absolutely unrelated entities. It is in this respect that native Korean spirituality, as it appeared in the shamanistic form of worship, was essentially non-dualistic. Spiritual blessings and material well-being were not separable from each other; yet, on the other hand, the spiritual dimension--i.e., the concern for supernatural powers--was deeply rooted in man's daily life within the material world. Worship was not considered as a detached ritual that separates the sacred from the secular, the holy form the profane, and spirit from matter. Rather, worship for the ancient Koreans was an intensive way of expressing their daily concerns and an extensive way of relating the spiritual dimension (or to a supernatural power).

4. The significance of ancestor worship

The Confucian tradition has been the most important religious heritage providing a moral foundation for ancestor worship. The moral aspect of ancestor worship has, in turn, been considered as probably the most important reason for preserving ancestor worship in most East Asian countries. The inextricable interweaving of Confucian morality with ancestor worship is exemplified in the concept of "filial piety" (Hsiao, Hyo, 孝). Filial piety, as the essential part of the Confucian moral system, is not limited to serving one's parents only while they are living, but extends to them even after they die. Thus, ancestor worship has become the most effective ritual expressing filial piety for the dead. For the Confucianists, life and death should not affect one's filial piety because filial piety is the foundation upon which man's moral cultivation rests. Furthermore, while the process of moral self-cultivation starts with the practice of filial piety, there can be no justification for the cessation of one's moral practices upon the death of one's parents. Man as a moral being must be able to respect and venerate his ancestors and to return to the roots of his existence. The idea of "returning to the origin" (pan si, 反始), and the feeling of "gratefulness" (po un, 報恩) comprise the foundation of filial piety.

Ancestor worship is a ritualization of the moral significance of filial piety. Both the moral dimension and the ritual dimension of filial piety are intrinsically related to each other; man's moral quality and his moral behavior are inseparable from one another. The relationship between morality and ritual is well expressed in the Confucian idea of "li" (子豊 propriety), which connotes the union of the inner moral awareness and the outer form of expression. Expression must not be understood simply in terms of communication in conveying one's moral quality to others. Rather, the Confucian significance of li lies in the concrete form of self-cultivation (hsiu, 修 , that it evokes. Li is not only a form of expressing one's moral quality, but more importantly, a means of enhancing it. In this respect, Confucian morality starts and ends with li. And, in particulars, filial piety also starts with li and ends with li. The relationship between li and filial piety was best expressed in the following statements from The Analects.

When parents are alive, serve them according to the rules of propriety. When they die, bury them according to rules of propriety and sacrifice to them according to the rules of propriety.

(The Analects. 2:5, Wing-tsit Chan's translation.)[9]

The above statements clearly indicate the "propriety" (li, 禮) in connection with filial piety, is to be practiced in three different states of man: life, death, and after death. And li penetrates all three of these states.

In order for us to have a better understanding of the Confucian view of man, we must survey the pre-Confucian view of man as held in ancient

China. Man is composed of the earthly aspect of the soul (p'o, 魄) and its heavenly aspect (hun, 魂). Hun is understood as the spirit of man's vital force that is expressed in man's intelligence and power of breathing. P'o, on the other hand, is the spirit of man's physical nature expressed in bodily movements.[10] When a man, dies p'o returns to the earth and hun disperses, as it were, into the air. It is not clear, in fact, where this hun goes. But what is the status of this hun in heaven? It was believed that hun is not an eternal entity, but that it gradually dissipates. In the light of the above considerations, it may be very difficult to make a definitive statement regarding the state of an ancestor. As Wing-tsit Chan rightly argues, the form of an ancestor has also changed from a personal form of ti (帝 , Lord) or Shang ti (上 帝 , the Lord on high) to an impersonal form of moral power:

> During the Shang, great ancestors were either identified with the Lord, or considered as mediators through whom requests were made to the Lord. In the Chou, they were still influential but, as in the case of Heaven, their influence was exerted not through power but through their moral example and inspiration.[11]

Here we see a process of transformation of the idea of the ancestor from the Shang to the Chou Dynasty. During the Chou Dynasty ancestors were not directly involved in human affairs. The only way in which the spiritual beings and human affairs could be related was through the initiative of the moral actions of human beings. In other words, the power of moral virtue was the essential force that relates man to the spiritual beings and vice versa. Thus, it was not considered that an ancestor would act upon human affairs on an arbitrary basis: "I have heard that spiritual beings are not endeared to man as such but cleave only to virtue."[12] During the time of Confucius, the cosmological and ontological speculations on ancestor worship were related to each other merely on a moral basis. Confucius himself was not deeply interested in speculating upon matters such as "spiritual beings" or the life after death. "If we are not yet able to serve man, how can we serve spiritual beings?" "...if we do not yet know about life, how can we know about death?"[13] Due to its lack of cosmological speculation, early Confucian anthropology was mainly occupied with discussions of the moral aspect of human nature rather than with the cosmological or an ontological significance of human beings. Although filial piety was considered the foundation of Confucian morality, it did not have the broader implication of man's relationship to the universe (cosmology) or of the formation of his being (ontology). Filial piety, of course, affirms the intrinsic ontological unity between parents and children; however, this sort of unity was mainly a biological one rather than an ontological unity. The ontological questions concerning the formation of being,--e.g., li (理 , principle) and ch'i (氣 , material force), were not fully developed until the Neo-Confucian era. The cosmological speculations concerning the ideas of t'ai chi, yin-yang, and wu hsing were not directly related to the view of man (anthropology) in the early Confucian tradition. Instead, the early Confucian anthropology was mainly based upon the moral significance of man. Because of this early Confucian influence, ancestor worship had gained moral significance but lost much of its cosmological significance. Even during the Neo-Confucian period, the cosmological significance of ancestor worship was still poorly developed because the Neo-Confucian ideas of ch'i (氣 , material force) and li (理 , principle) were not related to the idea of gods and spiritual beings. Most Neo-Confucian scholars did not accept the idea of the permanent existence of the departed spirit of an ancestor. Rather, the spirit and gods were nothing but phenomena of the expansion and contraction of the material force (ch'i, 氣).[14] The generation of a human being was also explained in terms of the condensation and dispersion of hun (魂) and Kuei (鬼).[15] A departed spirit, in this respect, was nothing but the result of the movements of the expansion and contraction of the material force (ch'i). A human being is also composed of li and ch'i; but since li does not condense or disperse, the condensation and dispersion of ch'i in the form of hun and p'o results in life and death. If we accept this Neo-Confucian assumption regarding the beginning and the end of life, we can see no convincing reason for believing that a departed spirit remains forever. Thus ancestor worship, even for the Neo-Confucianists, had little cosmological or ontological significance, and its moral significance was still the dominant aspect of ancestor worship. If we accept the principle, however, that filial piety must not be confined to the realm of the living but extends to that of the dead as well, we are then constrained to develop a coherent cosmology that can provide sufficient cosmological and ontological grounds for the moral practice. The lack of a cosmological dimension in ancestor worship, however, allowed the Confucian tradition to fuse with such a native Korean tradition as shamanism. One of the most significant contributions that the native folk religious traditions made to ancestor worship was the provision of rich cosmological speculations relevant to it. The Confucian tradition during the Yi dynasty was rigidly following the Chu Hsi (朱 熹 , 1130-1200) line of Neo-Confucianism. Although the ancestor worship ceremony was already well structured in accordance with Chu Hsi's "<u>Chu-tzu chia-li</u>" (朱子家禮), the popularizing of ancestor worship in Korea drew upon shamanistic motives. Specifically, shamanism played an important role in providing an adequate world view for ancestor worship. The shamanistic world view provided an effective way of relating life to death, and the world of a departed spirit to the world of man. Ancestors were supposed to possess the power to create calamities for their descendants or to give them blessings. Thus ancestor worship, with its moral, ritual, and cosmological aspects, now (during the Yi Dynasty) became a rich religious form of worship in Korea. Ancestor worship was no longer a ritual exclusively belonging to the Confucian tradition, but rather it was the most important and popular family ritual for all Koreans regardless of their religious affiliations, until Christianity was introduced. Thus ancestor worship was the most well-accepted religious ritual among the Koreans.

Another important reason for the popularization of ancestor worship was its ritual significance. As we noted earlier, the most ancient Korean form of worship was one that maintained the double aspect of ritual: the sacred ritual itself and the secular play. This double aspect was also apparent in the form of Korean ancestor worship, which was conducted not only with an attitude of utmost seriousness toward the departed spirits, but also with celebration as an important occasion for the reunion of families and relatives. In this respect, ancestor worship has played an important social role in maintaining family unity.

Such unity was maintained in two different dimensions: 1) that of the unity between the ancestors and the descendants of a family (a vertical unity); and 2) that of the unity among the living family members (a horizontal unity). The relationships among the contemporary members of a family and their relatives (the horizontal aspect) and those between the ancestors and their descendants (the vertical aspects) were not separable. The horizontal unity of a family was based upon its vertical unity, and the continuation of the vertical unity was dependent upon the horizontal unity of a family. Ancestor worship could satisfy both needs, the vertical and the horizontal, by providing sacred <u>ritual</u> for the ancestors and secular <u>play</u> for the members of the family. In so doing, ancestor worship became the focal point of family rituals and activities. One may thus conclude that the ritual function of ancestor worship in Korea has created the structural unity of the family.

The interdependency of the vertical and horizontal unities, however, can be effectively achieved only when ancestor worship develops cogent cosmological speculation regarding the power and influence of ancestors over their descendants. The moral dimensions of ancestor worship must be rooted in adequate cosmological and ontological speculation. The Korean form of ancestor worship was, in fact, able to maintain such cosmological speculation mainly by combining the native religious traditions, including those of shamanism, with the Confucian morality of ancestor worship.

Notes

[1] Ancestor worship has been studied from various perspectives including those of anthropology and sociology. We, should not ignore or neglect the fact however, that ancestor worship is essentially a religious phenomenon as E.B. Tylor has already convincingly argued. For the religious significance of ancestor worship, see Meyer Fortes, "An Introductory Commentary," in Ancestor, William H. Newell (ed.) (Hague, Paris: Mouton Press, 1976), pp. 1-16.

[2] The Cronicles of the Three-Kingdoms (三國志, 魏志, 東夷傳).

[3] These characteristics are drawn from Yu Tong-sik's significant study on Korean shamanism. Minsok Chongyo wa Hanguk Munhwa (民俗宗教와韓國文化) (Seoul; Hyondae Sasang Sa (現代 思想社), 1978).

[4] The concept of worship is comprehensively discussed in the article "Worship" in The New Encyclopaedia Britannica. Although the general concept of worship as defined in this article does not provide an adequate conceptual tool for ancestor worship, it does delineate a useful way of understanding the formal categories of worship.

[5] Samguksagi (三國史記). See also Yu Hong-yol (柳洪烈), 'Hanguk Samyo ui Palsaenge Taehan Il Koch'al," Hanguk Hak Yongu Ch'ongso(韓國祠廟發生 에對한一考察 , 韓國學叢書), Vol. 1 (Seoul: Sung jin Munhwa San (成進文化社), 1971), p. 214.

[6] Yu Tong-sik (柳東植), Minsok Chongyo wa Hanguk Munhwa (Seoul: Hyondae Sasang Sa, 1978), pp. 151-52.

[7] Ibid., pp. 155-56.

[8] Samgukyusa (三國遺事).

[9] Wing-tsit Chan, A Source Book in Chinese Philosophy (Princeton: Princeton Univ. Press, 1963), p. 23.

[10] The Book of History translated in ibid., p. 12.

[11] Ibid., p. 4.

[12] The Book of Odes, Wing-tsit Chan's translation, ibid., p. 11.

[13] The Analects, 11:11, Wing-tsit Chan's translation, ibid., p. 36.

[14] Chu Jae-young (朱在用), Sonyu ui Ch'on ju Sasang Kwa Chesa Mun je (先儒의天主思想과祭祀問題) (Seoul: Kyonghuang Chap ji Sa (京鄉 雜誌社) 1950), p.263.

[15] Ibid., pp. 263-64

Chapter II

Ancestor Worship: From the Perspective of Korean Church History

Myung Hyuk Kim

<u>Confucian culture</u>

As H. Richard Niebuhr has well pointed out, the relationship between Christ and culture has been "an enduring problem" throughout the history of Christian expansion.[1] When Christianity was introduced into the land of Korea about 200 years ago, the initial problem was the conflict between the Christian, God-centered way of life and the Confucian, man-centered way of socio-politico-ethical life.

The Korean culture during the last quarter of the 18th century, when Roman Catholic Christianity was first introduced, was thoroughly saturated with Confucianism, which focused upon the life principles of patriotic loyalty (忠) and filial piety (孝). As a national "religion" or policy of the Yi Dynasty, Confucianism espoused a basic ethical principle as well as a pragmatic socio-political policy. To honor filial piety, regarded as the most fundamental and integral ethical principle of Confucianism, was to follow the Mandate of Heaven (天命) and thus to reach the union of Heaven and man (天人合一), the ideal state of man. It was also intended to bring unity and harmony into the large family system and socio-political stability to the nation.

Filial piety was practiced through propriety and rite (礼), to both the living and the deceased (the ancestors).[2] Propriety occupied such an important position in the Confucian culture that Confucianism has often been called a culture of propriety system (礼制文化). Besides the basic ethical motivation to express and return filial gratitude to ancestors and to follow the Mandate of Heaven (天命), there was also a religious element attached to the ancestor honoring rite. Even though Confucius did not teach the immortality of the soul or the doctrine of the afterlife, the Confucian tradition taught that when a man dies his soul (魂氣)

ascends to heaven and his form (形魄) goes down to earth, and that the two are united in the ancestor worship ceremony .[3] Yi Yulgok (李栗谷), a saintly Confucian scholar (1536-1583), once stressed the necessity of ancestor worship on the basis of such a religious belief.

> When a man dies, his soul (鬼) might be said either to exist or not exist; for a soul exists with sincere devotion (誠) while it dissolves without devotion... When a man's soul (精氣) has been separated after death and has not yet dissolved, it can still be moved and elevated (感格) and united (聚合) through my sincere devotion (誠) ... Even after a man's soul has dissolved, his reason (理) does not dissolve; and his reason could be moved and elevated (感格) ... This is why descendants remember their ancestors and perform ceremonies in an utterly devoted manner.[4]

The ancestor worship ceremony gradually came to be accompanied by yet another religious idea, that of reward and blessing. It was believed that the faithful practice of filial piety and steadfast performance of the ancestor worship ceremonies would please Heaven and bestow heavenly blessings. Moreover, it was commonly believed that the deceased souls themselves, not Heaven, had the power to bless their descendants. Thus the deceased souls stepped into the position of deities and became objects of worship.[5]

Catholic Christianity

Catholic Christianity was not propagated in Korea by foreign missionaries. It was introduced by Korean scholars through their contacts with Christian literature obtained in Peking. Matteo Ricci, a Jesuit apostle to China, established his residence in Peking in 1601 and propagated Jesuit Christianity by introducing western science and publishing Christian literature. In His True Doctrine of the Lord of Heaven (天主實義), which appeared in 1601, Ricci avoided all negative attitudes toward Confucianism and its culture; rather he took it to be a preparation for Christianity. His mission policy was that of accommodation through learning.[6]

It was then customary for the King of Korea to send an annual envoy to Peking to present compliments and gifts to the Emperor of China.

Some of these members of the delegation came into contact with Matteo Ricci and his successors. In 1631, Chong To Wong (鄭斗源), a member of the annual embassy, brought back to Korea many books including Ricci's True Doctrine. The books thus imported to the Korean capital, however, received very little attention.[7]

It was not until almost the end of the 18th century that Catholic Christianity began to be rooted in the land of Korea. In 1777, a few celebrated scholars, such as Chong Yak Chon (丁若銓) and Kwon Chyol Sin (权哲身), became interested in the new doctrines, began to expound them, and commenced practicing the precepts of the Christian books. And in the winter of 1783, one of the annual embassy members, a young man by the name of Yi Sung Hun (李承薰) went to the Peking delegation. While in the imperial capital, he was converted and baptized. He was given the name of Peter, for it was hoped that he would become the first stone of the Korean Church. Peter Yi returned to Korea in the spring of 1784 and baptized his friend Yi Tok Cho (李德祚).[8] The year of 1784 is thus generally regarded as the founding date of the Roman Catholic Church in Korea.[9]

The Catholic teaching that was transmitted to Korea in 1784 was not the same as Ricci's. Matteo Ricci and his Jesuit mission had adopted an accommodation mission policy regarding ancestor worship merely as a civil ceremony. Both the Franciscan and Dominican missions, however, regarded the Confucian ancestor worship as religious and superstitious. Accordingly, the two missions sent a petition to Rome and won over Pope Benedictus XIV, who made it clear in 1742 that the Confucian ceremony of ancestor worship was not permissible in the Catholic Church. The Chinese Church followed the new instruction as well and as a result met with great difficulties and even persecution in 1784.[10]

In fact, the infant Korean Church plunged into difficulties from the very beginning, for she took a critical attitude towards Confucianism and especially its ancestor worship ceremony. Thomas Kim Pum Wu (金範禹) was the first victim, persecuted on the charge of burning his ancestral tablets. In 1970, the infant Korean Church sent one of its members to Peking to consult about the critical matter of ancestor worship and requesting that Bishop Alexandre de Goves send a priest to Korea. The messenger returned with the assurance and promise of the Bishop that an ordained man would be forthcoming. He was also instructed to make it known that the worship of ancestors was inconsistent with the doctrine of the Church. In accordance with Govea's prohibition of such worship, zealous Christian converts tore down their ancestral tablets and set them on fire. The consequence was the inauguration of systematic persecution.[11]

<u>Conflict and persecution</u>

Toward the close of the 18th century in Chulado, a southern Province of Korea, in the town of Jin San, there was a man of noble class by the name of Yun Chi Chyong (尹 持 忠,), who was converted in 1786 when he was 28 years old. In the summer of 1791, his mother died; and during the funeral period he refused to make ancestral tablets or to offer sacrifices to ancestors. This act stimulated a great commotion among his relatives and drew severe criticisms from them. Petitions were sent to the King. Yun Chi Chyong was finally brought to trial in a provincial court in October of that year. He was tortured and is reported to have said the following:

> Since I accepted the Heavenly Lord (天主) to be my great
> parent (大 父 母), it would be neither right nor honoring not
> to follow the order of the Heavenly Lord. Since the religion of
> the Heavenly Lord prohibits making a wooden tablet (神主),
> I buried it under the ground. I would rather do wrong to my
> deceased mother than to the Heavenly Lord.[12]

One investigator of Yun's experience, extolling Yun's pertinacity in following the Catholic teaching at the cost of disobeying the orders of the King or parents, wrote that . . .

> in every word he honors the teaching of the Heavenly Lord.
> It might be right for him to disobey the order of the King or
> the parent. It would never be right, however, to disobey the
> teaching of the Heavenly Lord even under the severest
> punishment. Uyn would have taken it as an honor to be
> beheaded.[13]

On receiving a report of Yun's trial and many critical petitions, the King was finally persuaded to render a sentence of execution. And in December of 1791, Yun Chi Chyong and Kwun Syang Yen (权 尚 然), his nephew, who also refused to offer sacrifices, were beheaded. This event is known as the <u>Shin</u> <u>hae</u> (辛 亥) Persecution, for it happened in the <u>Shin</u> <u>hae</u> year of 1791.

Even a priest from China, James Chu Moon Mo (周 文 謨), who was sent from Peking to Korea in 1794, was not exempted; for he too was beheaded in 1801 on charges of both religious heresy, for denying filial piety and abolishing sacrifice to ancestors, and political conspiracy against the nation. Acting under the impulse of such a tense situation, a certain Korean Catholic by the name of Whang Sa Young (黃 嗣 永) wrote a letter to the Bishop of Peking, in which he proposed an appeal to the Christian nations in Europe to send sixty or seventy thousand soldiers to conquer Korea. This document, which was discovered by a government agent, resulted in the strict enforcement of the anti-Christian edicts and an intensification of the persecution.[14] Now Catholic Christianity was regarded as a perverse religion standing against filial piety and patriotic loyalty. It was even suspected of revolutionary intentions against the nation. Thus, the Korean Catholic Church suffered persecution at the hands of the government in the years 1815, 1819, 1827, and 1839, and finally again in 1866.

<u>A new approach</u>

In the mid-Twentieth Century, the burning issue of ancestor worship in China was dealt with by Rome from a new perspective. On December 18th of 1939, the newly elected pope Pius XII issued an encyclical on the Chinese custom of ancestor worship, in which he declared that in a modern age in which the spirit of traditional customs has greatly changed, Confucian ancestor worship should be regarded merely as a civil rite to express filial affection to ancestors.[15] In 1940, the Korean Catholic Church adopted a rather tolerant attitude toward traditional ancestral worship, allowing such behavior as bowing in front of a corpse, a tomb, or a picture of the deceased; burning incense in front of a corpse or at the ancestral worship; and preparing and offering foods in memory of the deceased.[16]

The Second Vatican Council (1962-65) reaffirmed this tolerant attitude towards other religious traditions. The Constitution on the Sacred Liturgy (section 37) reads as follows:

> Even in the liturgy, the Church has no wish to impose a rigid uniformity in matters which do not involve the faith or the good of the whole community. Rather she respects and fosters the spiritual adornments and gifts of the various races and peoples. Anything in their way of life that is not indissolubly bound up with superstition and error she studies with sympathy and, if possible, preserves intact. Sometimes in fact she admits such things into the liturgy inself, as long as they harmonize with its true and authentic spirit.[17]

The traditional Roman Catholic teaching on purgatory in a way has justified Confucian ancestral worship, since it has taught us to pray for the dead.[18] Today the Korean Catholic allows bowing, burning incense in front of a corpse or a picture, and offering prayers for the dead during the funeral service and on the 3rd, 7th, and 30th days after death. The Church has even set a day, the 2nd of November, as a time of memorial and visiting ancestral graves.[19]

Protestant Christianity

As was the case with Catholic Christianity, Protestant Christianity in Korea was not started by foreign missionaries. It was introduced and planted by Korean merchants through their contacts with Protestant missionaries residing in Manchuria. In 1878, the So brothers, Sang Yun (徐相崙) and Sang U (徐相佑) (also known as Kyong Jo, 景祚), went to Manchuria to peddle merchandise and came into contact with John Ross and John MacIntyre, Scotch Presbyterian missionaries. They were converted and the elder brother Sang Yun was baptized by John Ross in 1879. So Sang Yun went to Mukden with Ross to assist in Bible translation and printing, while the younger brother returned home. Sang Yun later returned to Korea as a colporteur, smuggled translated portions of the New Testament into his home village in Uiju, and settled in Sorae in Hwanghae Province in 1883. Thus So Sang Yun became instrumental in the conversion of his neighbors and scattered the seed of the Gospel through the northwest regions of Korea. There was therefore already a handful of Protestant Christians in Korea when the American missionaries entered the country in 1884 and in 1885.[20]

Now the infant Korean Protestant Church faced the same puzzling problem about ancestor worship as the Catholic Church had faced a hundred years before. The first Korean convert was secretly baptized and his conversion was not made known even to his family. Yet his neglect of his religious duties soon placed him under public suspicion. It was a critical moment, for the first Protestant missionaries in Korea had to decide the very important question of their policy toward the custom of ancestral worship. Should it be conformity and compromise, or rejection? The missionaries at once adopted the latter course. Ancestor worship was now clearly declared to be contrary to Christian teaching.[21] One of the very interesting methods used in settling the question and reaching a definite conclusion was that of a questionnaire administered through a democratic procedure. A missionary sent out papers to the Christians and asked them to write down their views of the practice. The unanimous opinion was that ancestor worship was contrary to New Testament teachings and that offering sacrifice was foolish. One of them said: "For me, of course, I must remember my parents, but offering sacrifice to them is, I know, foolishness."[22]

There were rules promulgated in the Korean Church for the catechumens to adopt and profess to obey at baptism. The first of the seven rules used during the period from 1891 to 1897 read as follows: "Since the most High God hates the glorifying and worshiping of spirits, follow not the custom of the honoring of ancestral spirits, but worship and obey God alone."[23]

Shrine worship

During the last decade of the 36-year Japanese occupation of Korea (1910-45), the Korean Protestant Church faced the more difficult problem of shrine worship (神 社 参 拜). The Japanese government, beginning around 1932, tried to impose shrine worship upon every school and church in Korea. While the Japanese people understood shrine worship to be a religious ceremony involving the worship of ancestral gods and the emperor god, the Japanese government officials in Korea tried to persuade the Korean people to take it as a civil and national ceremony and forced them to participate in the shrine worship ceremony.[24] Missionaries as well as Korean church leaders expressed opposition to the Japanese imposition of shrine worship and thereby drew great difficulties upon themselves.   On December 30, 1935, a Japanese official in charge of education summoned a number of school principals (missionaries) and admonished them in the following words:

> The Shrine is a place where the spirits of our national father
> and veteran statesmen are dedicated; it is a public institution
> toward which we express our respect and reverence ...From
> an educational viewpoint it is necessary to worship such
> consecrated spirits, for it is an essence of national morality...
> Therefore, shrine worship is nothing more than a practical
> discipline of respect and reverence to ancestors.[25]

Instead of complying with the Japanese enforcement of shrine worship, school principals (especially of the Presbyterian missions) decided to leave their schools or close them.   By February of 1938, 18 schools under both the northern and southern Presbyterian missions were closed. In response, the Japanese government became more adamant in enforcing shrine worship upon the Korean Church. In September of 1938, Japanese police officials forced the Presbyterian General Assembly to adopt shrine worship as a patriotic national ceremony. Under a war-like police threat, Hong Taek Ki (洪澤麒), the Chairman of the Assembly, was trembling as he illegally announced the adoption. The adopted motion was recorded as follows: "We understand that shrine worship is not a religion and is not contrary to Christian doctrine. Realizing that it is a patriotic national ceremony, we have decided to take the lead in participating in shrine worship."[26] In spite of such an imposed resolution, the Korean Church (especially its Presbyterian membership) stood resolutely opposed to the Japanese enforcement of shrine worship and experienced many sufferings.

<u>Recent trends</u>

The Korean Presbyterian Church in general endured much suffering and faced many persecutions because of her strong opposition both to Confucian ancestor worship and to Japanese shrine worship. Many were imprisoned and even suffered martyrdom.

Even today some new converts face the persistent problem of ancestor worship, for the Confucian tradition dies hard even in a modernized age. Local pastors find it necessary to take counsel with some of the new converts on the annoying problem.

The Reverend Yonggi Cho, pastor of the famed mammoth Full Gospel Central Church in Seoul, gave some rather tolerant advice to a certain new convert with a strong Confucian background who was troubled with the problem of ancestor worship in 1977. In a public sermon delivered on November 30, 1979, the Reverend Cho expounded on the subject with an illustration of the counsel he gave to the new convert:

Ancestor worship (父母祭祀) is nothing but honoring one's parents. I do not understand why people say that it is idol worship... Parents are parents whether they are alive or dead. Isn't our custom to visit our living parents and prepare food for them? ...It is quite natural then that we think of our deceased parents on such days as their birth or death. It is quite all right to prepare food thinking of our deceased parents as if they were present, to erect a cross instead of an ancestral tablet, and to bow down... We honor our parents with bowing down. It is not an idol... Our deceased parents have gone either to heaven or hell. Even though they have gone to hell, they are our parents. Having an affectionate remembrance of them is keeping God's commandment... The Apostle Paul was a great man. To the Jews he became like a Jew to win Jews. To those under the law he became as one under the law. To those outside the law he became as one outside the law that he might win those outside the law... Thus, to perform ancestral worship (祭祀) is really a good thing. In the past we performed sacrificial rites to God.

This sermon stimulated heated discussion and met with nationwide criticism. The Christian Weekly Press (Nov. 7, 1981) printed the critical remarks of ten Christian leaders, as follows: "We express our filial courtesy to our living parents. Deceased ones are not persons; and preparing food and bowing to them is contrary to the Commandment" (Prof. Chung Sung Koo). "What Christianity takes as important is the person. We believe in God as a person. Deceased parents, however, are not persons;... and bowing to impersonal beings is nonsense" (Rev. Chung Chin Kyung). "In 1 Corinthians 10:20 Paul said: 'What pagans sacrifice they offer to demons and not to God. I do not want you to be partners with demons'. Sacrificial rules are prescribed in the Scriptures. Ancestor worship is an idol worship" (Prof. Lee Jong Yune). "There have been two kinds of mission policy in Asia, accommodation and transformation. Whereas ancestor worship was tolerated in such countries as India, China, and Japan, it was discountenanced in Korea. The earliest missionary policy in Korea was that of transforming old customs. It rejected wine, tobacco, opium, divination, and ancestor worship. Though ancestor worship is a traditional cultural rite, it includes an idolatrous element and cannot be tolerated" (Prof. Kim Myung Hyuk). "Preparing food and bowing to one's deceased parents even without making an ancestral tablet is an obvious idolatry. Jesus himself abolished the Jewish sacrificial system and instituted a worship with prayers... Numerous men of faith have suffered because of this problem of ancestor worship. It would be a disgrace to them if we were to say that bowing without a tablet is not idolatry" (Prof. Chun Kyung Youn of Hankook Theological Seminary). "If there is a pastor who says that it is alright to prepare a sacrificial table and bow, he must be lacking in theological foundation" (Rev. Choi Hae Il). "Preparing food and bowing is contrary to theology and to the Bible (Rev. Choi Hoon).

Concluding remarks

Tradition dies hard. There is even a revival and resurgence of tradition in the Third World. Voices affirming tradition and the cultural heritage are widely heard both in the theological and political worlds. The Vancouver Assembly tried to affirm the religious traditional spirituality of the

Canadian Indians consonant with Biblical spirituality. Likewise, Professor Pyun Sun Whan, a noted Korean liberal theologian and a champion of dialogue with other religions, has recently expressed his affirmative view about ancestor worship in the Dong-A Ilbo (December 24, 1983), a most widely circulated daily news, as follows: "Ancestor worship is a social product of a large-family system. To express filial piety and perform sacrifices is to follow an ethic designated by Heaven. Ancestor worship is an expression of filial affection, not an idolatry." Mr. Jin Hee Lee, minister of Cultural Affairs and Information and spokesman of the Korean government, has also exhorted Christian leaders to take a rather affirmative attitude toward Korean culture; and it was he who proposed the task of the "Koreanization of Christianity" in a public speech to a gathering of Christian leaders on December 16, 1983.

It is time that we Evangelicals should be alerted to a full understanding of the relation between the Christian Gospel and secular culture and should provide clear-cut solutions in concrete situations. It would be well for us to realize the criticizing, transforming, and recreating function and power of the Gospel in various cultures as others have done throughout the history of Christianity.

Notes

[1]See H. Richard Niebuhr, Christ and Culture (New York: Harper, 1951), pp. 1ff.

[2]Confucius once said that "Honor through propriety when living; bury through funeral rites when dead; and perform ceremony through rites" (論語爲政：生事之以礼．死葬之以礼、祭之以礼).

[3]See Choi Ki Bock, A Study on the Confucian Ceremony of Mourning (儒教의 喪禮에 關한 硏究) (Sung Kyun Kwan Univ., 1979), pp. 128f.

4 栗谷全書 拾遺 卷위死生鬼神業．
Quoted by Choi Ki Bock, ibid., 129f.

[5]See Park Bong Bae, "Christianity and Ancestor Worship" (Korean) in Harold Hong et al (ed.), Church and Mission in Korea (C.L.S.K., 1963), pp. 201f.

[6]See Choi Such Woo, "Modern Korean Society and Roman Catholic Christianity" (Korean) in Soong Chun Journal 5 (1974), p. 422.

[7]L. George Paik, The History of Protestant Missions in Korea 1832-1910 (Seoul: Yonsei University Press, 1929 (1970)0, pp. 31f.

[8]Ibid., p. 32.

[9]See Choi Suck Woo, op. cit., p. 426.

[10]See Choi Suck Woo, op. cit., p. 428.

[11]See L. George Paik, op. cit. pp. 32f.

12 正祖實錄 卷三二 正祖 15年 11月 戊寅
Quoted by Choi Suck Woo, op. cit., p. 429.

[13]Idem.

[14]See L. George Paik, op. cit., pp. 34f.

[15]See Choo Jae Young, Confucian Concept of the Heavingly Lord and Ancestor Worship (Lorean) (Seoul: Kyung Hyang, 1958), p. 3.

[16]See Kang Youn Hee, "The Problem of Ancestor Worship in Christianity in Modern Korean Society," (Korean) Sa Mock 37 (1975, 1), pp. 100f.

[17]Walter M. Abbott (ed.), The Documents of Vatican II New York: Guild Press, 1966), p. 151.

[18]See Sebastian Bullough, Roman Catholicism (Harmond-worth: Penguin Books, (1963) p. 141: "The notion of purgatory and the notion of prayer for the dead go hand in hand: the 'communion of saints' unites the living with the dead in prayer."

[19]See Choo Jae Young, op. cit., p. 202.

[20]See L. George Paik, op. cit., pp. 51-54.

[21]See L. George Paik, op. cit., pp. 157f.

[22]See L. George Paik, op. cit., pp. 220f.

[23]See L. George Paik, op. cit., pp. 225f.

[24]See Kim Yang Sun, History of the Korean Church: Study of the Maesan Christian Culture (Korean: Christian Literature Co., 1971), pp. 172-76.

[25]Ibid., p. 180.

[26]Ibid., p. 189.

Chapter III

Ancestor Worship: From the Perspective of Confucianism and Catholicism

Ki-bok Ch'oe

Confucianism holds that all men are born good and that men, whether saints or fools, are all the same, as everyone comes from heaven and receives heaven's virtues and orders when he is born into this world. This is the basic view of man in Confucianism and constitutes the foundation of Confucianism's thought system. A problem that arises here is how to develop the good nature of a man to make him into a well-rounded person, namely a wise man or a saint. Confucianism is interested not in the philosophical aspect of "what a man is," but in an implemental and character-building aspect of "how a man can become a genuine man by fulfilling his inherent nature." Confucius, instead of expounding noble doctrines, preached the ideal that all men should become humane by practicing benevolence and stressed filial piety and brotherly love as the basis for implementing benevolence. Mencius also taught filial piety and brotherly love as the substance of benevolence and righteousness when he said: "The substance of benevolence is to honor one's parents, and that of righteousness is to respect one's elder brothers." Both Confucius and Mencius placed utmost importance on filial piety and brotherly love. The former advised that learning be practiced if there were occasion to do so after having implemented filial piety and brotherly love. According to the latter, on the other hand, "the essence of wisdom lies in understanding filial piety and brotherly love well and not abandoning them. And the substance of propriety lies in giving beautiful colours to filial piety and brotherly love, while that of pleasure lies in enjoying filial piety and brotherly love as well." Mencius also stated that "the way to Emperors Yao and Shun," who have the qualities of an ideal man under Confucianism," is nothing but filial piety and brotherly love." Ch'eng I-ch'uan had this to say: "The perfection of nature and fulfillment of order are necessarily founded on filial piety and brotherly love. Nature and order belong to the same stream as filial piety and brotherly love. One can perfect nature and fulfill order while practicing filial piety and brotherly love." As brotherly love can be included in filial piety and as the former may arise from the latter, filial piety constitutes "the foundation" and "the greatest virtue," of the implemental virtues of Confucianism. Mencius thus went as far as to accuse one who does not fulfill his filial duties as being neither an offspring nor a man.

The fundamental spirit of filial piety can be summarized in two acts. One is that of rewarding the origin from which one has received life. One cannot but reward his or her parents, the origin of his life, body, and spirit. And propriety denotes rewarding the origin. The other is the act of repaying the affections and favors that parents have given their sons and daughters. Parents pour their affections into and devote themselves to their sons and daughters, who, in turn, are the outcome of the sacrifices and devotions made by their parents. When one thinks about and appreciates such parental affections and kindnesses, one cannot but have a sense of gratitude and an impulse to repay his parents' favors.

Filial piety originating from rewarding the origin and repaying parents' favors expresses itself in three forms. First of all, it takes the form of preserving one's own body. If parents are compared to foundations or roots, children are then branches. If branches are hurt, trunk and roots are affected as well; therefore children ought to preserve their bodies, given by their parents, in good shape, and to take care of their bodies with a pious mind. Secondly, filial piety is shown in serving and respecting one's parents. Children should greet their parents every morning and evening, look after the condition of their clothes, food, and quarters, and honor them with pleasure. Thirdly, it expresses itself in upholding the teachings of one's parents and advancing in society. According to parental precepts children should learn and acquaint themselves with virtue, uphold the intentions of their parents, advance in society, and win respect from others, thereby offering glory to their parents.

Filial piety in Confucianism does not end when one's parents die, but the rewarding of the origin and repaying of parents' favors continue after their death in the form of funerals and memorial rites. Confucius urged men to "serve your parents while they are alive with decorum, bid farewell to them in funerals with decorum, and remember them in memorial rites with decorum as well." The Canon of Filial Piety says: "To serve one's parents with respect and affection while they are alive and to remember them with sorrow and solemnity after their death with services provided to them as if they were alive fulfills the duties of a man including that of filial piety." In Confucianism importance is thus placed on serving one's parents after death as much as on doing so during their lifetime; and as for serving them after death as if they were alive it rates this as the culmination of filial piety. The significance of the ancestral rite lies in its continuing of the filial piety of rewarding the origin and repaying parents' favors by extending it to dead parents in the same manner as one would have done while they were alive.

"An ancestral rite denotes an extension of filial piety by serving the dead continuously. An ancestral rite therefore is conducted not with reluctance, but with wholeheartedness. An ancestral rite is held to repay the origin and repay the benevolence one has received."

The culmination of filial piety in Confucianism calls for serving one's parents during their lifetime as if one served Heaven and having them share Heaven when ancestral memorial rites are held after their death. Having one's ancestors share Heaven does not imply that one places Heaven and ancestors on the same level or identifies ancestors with Heaven. Sacrifices offered to Heaven were different from those offered to ancestors. It was reasoned that as ancestors originated from Heaven while being the origin of life for their offspring, rewarding ancestors, the origin, for a long time after their death through ancestral rites can reward Heaven, the origin of ancestors, as well. Thus, the concept of having ancestors share Heaven came about. This applies to ordinary citizens.

A king performed the act of rewarding the origin by holding a special rite to Heaven as the representative of his entire people. Confucianism thus holds that the most important qualities are benevolence and filial piety, the virtues of men' that one fulfills his filial piety to heaven through such piety to his or her parents; and that the significance of ancestral rites, men's obligations, lies in the rewarding of one's ancestors, the origin of his life, and Heaven for a long time after their death. In Confucianism religious thought is so closely related to ancestral worship that it can be called "a two deities religion of worshiping Heaven and ancestors"; and in it ethics and religion "are one and two, and two and one at the same time."

More important than anything else in Confucian rites are sincerity and respect, depending on the degree to which communion with God or enjoyment by God can be determined. Accordingly, one has to purify himself and demonstrate his sincerity before holding a rite. One purifies oneself thoroughly with sincerity, and precepts go; and when one feels as if the spirit resides just above, on the left and right side, and its voice is heard, then is the time when one's sincerity is received by God. If a rite is held at such a moment, it is said, the spirit can enjoy it. Confucius said that "men in holding rites should assume that the spirit is indeed there"; that however spectacular a rite may be it is meaningless and not worthy of being seen if devoid of sincerity; and going a step further, that nothing is significant if it is not accompanied by sincerity.

What are the procedures of Confucian rites and their symbolic meanings? To begin with, the Master of Rites bows to an ancestral tablet when it is taken out of a shrine as he did when the ancestor involved was alive; and he then invokes the soul by burning incense and pouring liquor. These are expressions of an urgent desire to have the soul at the spot. Upon feeling the residence of the soul nearby, the Master of Rites offers liquor and food in a symbolic gesture of sincerity and respect. The reading of a ritual prayer follows, in which the soul is called upon to enjoy the sacrifices offered as a means of expressing affection. A ritual prayer is read in a manner as though conversing with one's parents while they were alive, expressing yearning and honoring. Cups are filled with liquor for the second and third times while following a ritual prayer; and then all leave the room where the rite is observed so that the soul may enjoy the sacrifices. This is a plain expression of the offsprings' urgent wish that the ancestor appreciate their sincerity and devotion; it is a ritual by which mourners are led to believe that the soul responds to their wish. After a while the mourners enter the room again, withdraw a bowl of soup and serve tea, and then bid farewell to the soul by bowing. The ancestral tablet is then returned to the shrine and a tablet made of paper is burned. Liquor and food used for an ancestral rite are shared by families and relatives. This can be described as a sort of affection festival designed to share identity with the soul and promote harmony among family members and relatives.

The significance of a Confucian ancestral rite lies in fulfilling one's filial duties by remembering one's ancestors, rewarding the origin, and repaying favors given by ancestors, and not in the enjoyment of a rite by the soul. Neither is it designed to seek good fortune. Confucianism nevertheless neither denies nor rejects fortune, but holds that a wise man is bound to enjoy fortune by holding an ancestral rite.

"An ancestral rite offered by a wise man is necessarily rewarded by fortune. The fortune referred to here does not denote ordinary fortune, but a state of being equipped--which means that one adapts oneself to all duties. In other words, one fulfills inwardly his sincerity to the fullest extent and outwardly abides by duties... No other fortune is sought for oneself and this is the mind of a filial son or daughter."

Fortune as referred to in Confucianism is the faithful fulfillment of one's duties. As the holding of an ancestral rite with extreme sincerity, according to Confucianism, is a faithful fulfillment of men's duties, the observation of the ancestral rite as such contains in itself fortune. In a nutshell, in Confucianism by conducting an ancestral rite one achieves oneness with the dead psychologically; faithfully fulfills benevolence and filial piety (which are ethically, the duties of children); and--going a step deeper--religiously worships Heaven.

The banning of ancestral rites themselves by Catholicism on the grounds that "materialistic foods cannot feed the soul and the offering of foods to the dead constitute an empty formality" is considered to have come about not because of the fundamental meanings of the Confucian ancestral rites, but because of a judgment based merely on their heterogeneous, symbolic rituals. This is evident in the following dialogue that took place between Bishop Gouvea and Yun Yuil:

Yi-il: The holding of an ancestral memorial service is designed to serve the dead as if one served a living parent. It renders the life of a Catholic convert very difficult not to be allowed to observe an ancestral memorial rite. Can't there be any way to overcome this hurdle?

Bishop: Catholicism attaches great importance to sincerity; and the offering of foods to the dead violates sincerity.

The ancestral tablet originally stemmed from a child who in a memorial rite was substituted for a dead ancestor. As neither portraits nor photographs were available in ancient times, they had no way of seeing the image of their parents in ancestral rites--with the result that their minds could not concentrate. Hence they regarded substitute children as spiritual images of their ancestors, to whom they offered sincerity and respect. The origin of the practice of using children as substitutes for ancestors in memorial rites lay--according to Pe Hu T'ung--in men's natural desire to have some images they can see. The book has the following paragraph:

The soul, having neither voice nor shape, cannot be seen anywhere, including the ceiling and the room in which he used to live. Nothing can be found but vessels that he used to employ. Being so hollow and lonely, one can find no object to which one can direct one's yearning and mourning. Accordingly, a child was made to sit and take food. If some sacrifices were consumed or scattered they were pleased, assuming that the ancestor being remembered would have eaten them. If the child were intoxicated they were also pleased, assuming that the soul of the ancestor had had enough drink.

Children who substituted for ancestors were selected from among the grandchildren of the dead, a grandson in case the deceased was a male and a granddaughter in case the deceased was a female. That the offspring of the dead were made to substitute for the dead reflects the belief that the life and spirit of the dead ancestor are handed down to his offspring. This also helped the offspring to recall and remember their dead ancestors. Substitute children were dressed in clothes worn by the dead, which can be interpreted as an expression of filial piety designed to recall and serve the dead with sincerity. The practice of having children seated at the altar came to an end after the Chou dynasty, when they were replaced by ancestral tablets.

An ancestral tablet contains two meanings: 1) One is the image of the invisible soul. Men needed some images in order to express their respect to their dead ancestors as they did while they were alive. This applies to other major religions as well. Buddhism deifies Buddha images, while Christianity uses crosses or portraits of Jesus Christ as a means by which believers concentrate their minds and worship God. In Confucianism, as mentioned above, they had children seated as substitutes for the dead inasmuch as neither portraits nor photographs were available; and these children were later replaced by ancestral tablets, which served as images of the soul. An ancestral tablet is accordingly an image of the soul, prepared as a visible image through which offspring may pay respect and express affection to the invisible soul of their dead ancestor. 2.) An ancestral tablet also serves as the resting place of the soul. Confucianism holds that it is irresponsible to let the soul loiter around without a resting place. As a result, they make a temporary silk tablet for the dead, which is replaced by a wooden ancestral tablet following the funeral services, prepared as a resting place for the soul.

Of the two meanings, more importance is attached to the image of the soul than to the resting place of the soul. This is the evident intent in the origin of the ancestral tablets and also in the practice in which the paper ancestral tablet used in a memorial rite as a substitute for a wooden tablet is burned as soon as the rite is over. Catholicism banned the use of ancestral tablets on the grounds that "an ancestral tablet cannot be called one's parents inasmuch as it is nothing but a piece of wood carved by a carpenter," and that "the soul of a man, who is dead, does not reside in anything physical." In its own interpretation, Catholicism stressed the meaning of the resting place more than that of the image of the soul. Such an interpretation appears to have been influenced by certain Dominicans and Franciscans, who found superstitious elements in the villagers' rites that were affected by Taoism and indigenous faith. Jesuit missionaries, on the other hand, permitted the use of ancestral tablets by interpreting them as the image rather than as the resting place of the soul. This was probably because Jesuit missionaries, thanks to their contact with Confucian Scholars who opposed superstition, appreciated the true Confucian meanings of ancestral rites and tablets.

Catholicism banned the Confucian ancestral rites in Korea viewing them as superstitions based upon the Western way of thinking that physical food cannot feed the soul, and that offering food to the dead is an empty formality--as can be seen from the fact that no foods are served to one while one is asleep. The decision was reached based not upon the fundamental meaning of Confucian ancestral rites--namely, to reward the origin for a long time after the death of ancestor--but upon heterogeneous rituals. In banning the use of ancestral tablets, Catholicism reasoned that tablets, pieces of wood made by carpenters, cannot be called one's parents; and that the soul of the dead cannot reside in anything physical. Such reasoning arose because an ancestral tablet was regarded as a resting place of the soul, instead of an image of the soul, whereas the latter was in fact more significant than the former. Underlying the prohibition of ancestral rites and tablets by Catholicism was a sense of superiority on the part of Europeans that cultures and thoughts other than those of Europeanized Christianity are inferior, and a lack of understanding of heterogeneous cultures and thought. The abolition of ancestral rites and tablets was received as a negation or destruction of traditional ethics and thought systems; and Catholic converts were regarded as unfilial sons and daughters and non-nationals. These attitudes resulted not only in bloodshed and the erection of a major obstacle to the propagation of Catholicism and its adaptation to local conditions, but also in the perception that Christianity is a European religion foreign to Orientals.

The historic lesson to be learned from the abolition of ancestral rites and tablets is that we, in our contact with other religions, should conduct more fundamental and serious studies into their theologies, and should do so with humility. All men originate from Heaven and are born good and identical. They are bound to express in one form or another their respect for Heaven and their parents, the origin of their life. Forms in which they express themselves can differ in accordance with the natural features, ways of thinking, culture, and history of a region. This can be likened to the fact that though men are identical by nature, they use different languages. It is necessary for us to study with humility how other cultures and religions express the pure nature of men as well as their merits, and to be courageous enough to accept that, for whomever possesses the truth, its foundation is the same. In this way alone we can make our own experience mature and rich, on the one hand, and help the other side to mature as well.

A Christianity that understands everything in the context of the work of salvation accomplished by God, in particular, ought to discern the profound divine providence of redemption with humility in the culture of other religions. Even if imperfect things were found in other religions as judged through the eyes of Christianity, a religion of revelation, we should try to remedy their faults slowly through patient dialogue. To reject other cultures and thoughts themselves might preserve the legitimacy and purity of Christianity, but would not bring the Good News to all. Confucianism, on the other hand, should not insist upon its absolute legitimacy, but should mature itself in the realm of religious thought through dialogue and intercourse with Christianity just as it saw the birth of Neo-Confucianism through contact with Taoism and Buddhism. It is hoped that the ban on ancestral rites and the consequent historic tragedy will serve the purpose of expediting Catholicism's adaptation to indigenous conditions, its evangelization of the nation, and its dialogue with other religions.

For sources and documentation on this essay, see the Korea Journal, August, 1984.

Chapter IV

Ancestor Worship: From the Perspective of an Early Protestant Christian

Pyun Young Tai

<u>What ancestor worship is</u>

I must first try my readers' patience by telling what so-called ancestor worship is. There are various versions of this rite in different lands, grouped under the same appellation. But, as I am ignorant of the forms in which it appears in other lands, my treatment of this subject cannot but be confined to that form prevalent in Korea. I do not know whether there are forms of ancestor worship in other countries that can be properly and justly be called such; but I do know that there is some sense of gross injustice in applying this term to that in this land, unless the word "worship" is used in its obsolete sense of "recognition of merit." Even with this construction of the word, the term is not well chosen or to the point, though it is divested of its slanderous sense by so construing it. Therefore, I am rather inclined to give it a new name suggestive of its intrinsic, underlying motive. I suggest that it ought to be termed "ancestor-commemoration," if there is no better name.

Ancestor worship in Korea dates back to times immemorial and has been observed by people, high and low, scholars and peasants, age after age, without a single break. It has been from the very start purely a memorial service. Before coming to discuss what ancestor worship actually is today, let me allocate a small space to its possible origin, its sanction and inculcation by Confucianism, and some remarks made on it by early Confucian scholars. If one should wish to grasp the origin of the rite graphically it would be necessary to imagine themselves back to a primitive age. There is the untouched primitive forest full of wild beasts; the rude log cabin, which is their whole world, holding every possible interest they care for and in which they feel secure from nocturnal attacks by panthers and tigers; a few patches of land surrounding their homestead, cleared not long ago, studded with the stumps of the felled trees.

To them the family seems all in all, the only refuge against every manner of attack from outside. The swarthy, tawny couple, the parents of the family, love, toil, and fight for their children, who look up to them not only as mere father and mother but also protectors, warriors, and heroes. A kind of hero-worship is mixed with and at the same time strengthens the natural reverence and affection due to their parents. At length, old age steals upon the senior members of the little group, and one day death suddenly claims one of them. What a grief! What a fear about the future! The most valiant of the community lies there pallid and dead! They cannot brook the thought of parting even with the dead body. They detain it in their home as long as it has any semblance of their brave father. Then they bury it away, very close to their home. At no meal can they escape the sense of painful vacancy at the table. The spoon, the chopsticks, the largest bowl, used by the deceased when living, are still there; but alas! the man is no more. Their uncontrollable grief overcomes them. One of them bursts into crying, quickly followed by the others, all throwing themselves on the floor. Grief finding thus free vent, they feel themselves a little soothed. With the return of calm, in their untutored hearts they feel that the tie of affection between the deceased and themselves is not broken and the spirit of the deceased seems to be with them still, there at the very table, in deep sympathy with them and even partaking of the meal in some invisible manner, characteristic of a ghost or spirit. They not only feel it natural that the portion for the man should be on the table as it was a few days ago while he was still living; but they instinctively shrink from the mere thought of non-provision of that portion as an act of flagrant ingratitude. We can well imagine, harking back to those days of the simplest human transactions, how strongly the memory of such an unutterable loss should hold them, and abide with them. It is quite natural, to think too, that this kind of drama should have happened in every primitive home in every land. This innocent, even fine, sentiment must have been the origin of ancestor worship the world over, though later developments have varied widely from one another on account of different surroundings and influences.

Now the long line of Chinese sages--culminating in the great master Confucius and followed by lesser but illustrious persons--saw that filial love is the seed of every virtue and tried to model a groove, for human conduct to follow, as it were, to prevent a man from falling, and in so doing to impress this master-virtue upon his mind in various ways, especially (as one of the many ways), by embodying it in a set of rites, which are now called ancestor worship. The stereotyped manner of prostration by way of humble obeisance made by the worshipers (you would fain call them so, though I would not), the unnatural mode of lamentation, the prescribed arrangement of oblation foods, the certain air of hypocrisy inherent in any set form, the insincere superstitions hanging around it--all have contributed to spoiling the innocent, beautiful, sincere manner of expressing one of the finest human sentiments indulged in by those naked, half savage, but right-hearted primitive men. The artificiality, which is so repulsive and compels us to be less tolerant than we ought to be, seems too much to leave adequate room for the play of natural sentiment. The form seems to strangle the very spirit that it is meant to convey. This set form has lived for several thousand years without a jot changed. This standpattism, this ignoble similarity, this want of individuality has been a great danger, if not the sole threat to the civilization of the East.

Nevertheless, what have we to infer? Despite all the uncouth, timeworn, grotesque manners of the rite, it is still meant to hold and, in the cases of traditional scholars and nearly the whole of the peasantry in the land, it actually does hold its original sentiment intact, though not without the alloys of drab dutifulness and keeping up to social respectability. One of our famous scholars remarked, "Food offering to our ancestors' spirits is significant in reminding us of our origin." Another said, "It is a commemoration." "Fall sets in, the frost sitting on the leaves," once remarked Mencius, the great Chinese thinker; "then men are suddenly in a yearning mood," thus justifying the offering made after the harvest. This offering we call "<u>shiche</u>," meaning "season offering," the offering tendered in the autumnal season. There is also another called "<u>chunshin</u>," any of an unfixed number of offerings, in the course of a year, of seasonal foods and fruits, without any fixed date, nor attended by usual ceremonies. On the other hand, the anniversary offering takes place with exact punctiliousness on the eve or, strictly speaking, in the small hours of the death-day of the dead. The death-day of any parent is called "ki-il" or "whi-il" connoting "a day painful to mention," "an unhappy day." Hence the offering on this occasion is known as "ki-che."

From first to last it must be remembered that we are examining here the form that ancestor worship took in Korea only, regardless of other forms in other places. Indeed, if the Encyclopaedia Britannica should be believed, it would be true beyond any doubt that, in China, the spirit of ancestor worship has greatly degenerated. A passage dealing with the subject runs thus:

> Ancestor worship in China has always been, and still is, worship in the strictest sense of the term. It is not a memorial service in simple honour of the dead; but sacrifices are offered and the whole ceremonial is performed that the spirits of former ancestors may be induced to extend their protection to them and secure to them as many as possible of the good things of the world.

Except for the evidence that the foregoing statement is entirely groundless, nothing can justify denial of the fact that ancestor worship in China has diverged from its honorable spirit and degenerated into mammonism. However far it may be from the above author's intention to evince prejudice against China simply because he can offer no better statement of the matter, his point here is to declare that whether this report is exact or not as regards the prevalent spirit of ancestor worship in China, the cleancut motive underlying the kindred rite in his own land (Korea) is absolutely free from any sordid incentive. No trace is to be found even among the most ignorant people that hints at any fear or greed in connection with this pure memorial service.

On the other hand, there are a multitude of reminders that substantiate the Britannica author's contention that it has been, and is, nothing less and nothing more than a memorial service. In this light alone, the strange phenomenon that a married son, when dead, is offered this self-same "worship" by his surviving father, can be rightly explained away.

Every family of landed property, as a rule, sets apart a portion of their land for the commemoration of their ancestors. Especially, in some northern provinces of the country, they call this dedicated land "bul-mang-tab." "Bul-mang" means "not forget," while "tab" denotes "a rice field"--that is, a field dedicated to the memorial service.

And if some observers of the rite should entertain the notion that Heaven will punish those who dare to neglect the filial duty of commemorating ancestors, this is no detached special superstitious dread arising only in connection with ancestor worship; it is instead a fresh confirmation of the general moral view held in the East that Heaven requites good with blessings and evil with calamities; for this arch-rite is regarded as an essential good and accordingly its breach as an evil.

As regards such further minor points as those raised about the ancestral tablet, their full treatment being forthcoming in one of the succeeding chapters, I shall forego discussion of them here in order to avoid needless repetition.

Idolatry defined

The second commandment of the Decalogue says:

Thou shalt not make unto thee a graven image, nor any likeness of anything that is in heaven above, or that is in the earth beneath, or that is in the water under the earth: thou shalt not bow down thyself unto them, nor serve them; for I, Jehovah, thy God, am a jealous God, visiting the iniquity of the fathers upon the children, and upon the third and upon the fourth generation of them that hate me; and showing loving kindness unto thousands of them that love me and keep my commandments.

This commandment opposes every visible form of idolatry, every worship of any visible image of something, human or otherwise. Very loosely and radically construed, this commandment even seems to frown upon the Eastern mode of salutation done to one's superiors by prostrating oneself upon the floor, for it may well be asked how the jealous Jehovah can put up with such excessive marks of respect paid to man, when it is manifest that He abhors any form of homage paid to a hand-made image? Thus, one might pass to the ironic extreme of supposing that carrying one's neck boltstraight before people should be made a fundamental condition of salvation. Putting aside, however, all of this almost ridiculous representation, let us try to find the true spirit in the law and see where we can go in this way of seeking.

This is what I see or what I hold that we ought to see in this particular law: Jehovah, the almighty God, is the only God whom man must tremblingly fear, lest he should go astray from Him. The perfection of humanity can be achieved only through Him who is the sole cause of humanity. He has created our thirst and He alone knows how to satisfy it. Therefore, it is only in their moments of perverted delusion that men dream of seeking satisfaction, rest, or peace entirely apart from the ways of Jehovah, or from His commandments. Keep His laws and fear Him only, is the decree. Do not go out and worship molten or wooden things out of superstitious fear or unjustifiable greed, instead of trusting your true God, your only Cause, your only Creator and Perfector. All of the blessings possible for you now and forever are inherent in your being one with your God by conforming to His laws; and all evil things possible for you will come to you only as consequences of your disobedience to Him.

What does the New Testament say, then, about idolatry? It being impossible to collect ample references to it from this part of the Bible, we must content ourselves with just a glimpse of its nature as shown by the great apostle to the gentiles. Inasmuch as he, Paul, was converted spiritually after Jesus was glorified, so much is he the more suitable as a prototype of those followers of Jesus Christ in succeeding generations than the other eleven apostles would be, whose faith sprang from their personal attachment to their master while He was still on earth. In Colossians 3:5 we read these words: "Put to death therefore your members which are upon the earth: fornication, uncleanness, passion, evil desire, and covetousness, which is idolatry." There seems to be a great jump in the conclusion that covetousness is idolatry. This is, however, decidedly an extended view of idolatry. With a little consideration it becomes evident, though, that the New Testament condemns every object as idolatry, invisible as well as visible, that possesses the human soul, usurping the place of God, while it is only the Old Testament that stipulates the visibility of the object of worship is one of the fundamental conditions of idolatry. Where there is covetousness there is no God. Therefore, it is an idolatry. Here is a man who puts money above God; money is then his idol. And suppose that a man, for the sake of his beloved woman, goes against certain laws of God; what is he but an idolater, his woman being his object of worship? If this view be carried to the extreme, every shade of sin is nothing but some form of idolatry--an ugly usurpation of the homage due to God. But since that kind of idolatry with a visible image as its object is still prevalent everywhere, let us not push too far this argument that every sinful deed is an idolatrous one, and that the single term "idolatry" covers the whole world of sins. Then let it suffice here for us to grasp a comprehensive idea of idolatry from the amalgamation of the two Old and New Testament statements about it.

What is denoted, then, by the Christian conception of "idolatry" has five distinct features, whatever form it may be in: Firstly, the idolized object is something besides God, and is therefore against God, leaving its worshiper only one way of choosing between it and God: either he has to be out of it to be with God, or he must remain in it and be without God.

Secondly, greed has been found to be one of the chief incentives for idol-worshipers. They worship it in order to satisfy their baser cravings-- such as for the birth of a son, for a long life, or for the recuperation of health. They betake themselves to it, not with their own education in view, but merely to secure some of the conveniences for their worldly life.

Thirdly, one of the features of idolatry, and by no means the least, is fear, which can obsess the whole being of the worshiper--a superstitious fear, unfounded except on mere emotion. It is easily observed that the whole service of any idol worship is prevaded by this cowardly feeling. If greed comprises the chief part of the motivation supporting idolatry, assuredly fear fills the remainder. Just as overbearing arrogance and fawning servility are usually found in the self-same character, so greed and fear go hand in hand. Idol-worshipers look upon the world as bristling with hostile spirits, whom they think must be appeased or cajoled rather than reasoned with, in order to avert any harm to their interests. This accumulated feeling of fear, haunting at every turn, finds vent in idol-worship, no less frequently than the release actuated by greed.

The fourth feature of idolatry is the fact that it is entirely unethical, and consequently irreligious; it is devoid of any moral tincture. The worshiper goes to the black power to bargain something out of it, not to be edified; to obtain certain things, not to invoke life-fire, so to speak. They do not mean to grow more beautiful and useful themselves as the result of their worship, but intend instead to surround themselves just as they are with things that they, as what they are, deem beautiful and useful. The idol has nothing to do with the education of its worshiper. Hence, his soul-growth is arrested and choked just because he has chosen it as his object of worship, which has no connection whatever with his spiritual evolution.

The last feature of idolatry, which needs least mention because it is almost self-evident, is that it involves a deified object of vision--an idol. Indeed, this feature ought to have been the foremost one, you might say. But in the ranking of importance it may as well be placed last, for it is quite immaterial whether the object is visualized or not, provided that it affects its worshiper's moral constitution in the manner set forth in the foregoing four features.

This is my picture of idolatry; I hope that this picture even if not exactly the same as yours, will pass before the mind's eye of many readers, who will spare a few minutes to contemplate this strange human phenomenon. And I hope, too, that I shall not be amiss in sketching out this rough contour of idolatry if I make it a touchstone against which to test so-called ancestor worship, in order to ascertain whether an ancient custom of the people has been rightly classified as a type of idolatry.

Unjust charge of idolatry

There are Christians who take ancestor worship in the fullest sense to be idolatry. But those are not also lacking, who hold ancestor worship to have no connection whatever with any form of idolatry. Lest our readers should mix that special form of ancestor worship practised in Korea with its other forms enacted in other lands, I will help to guard them against this confusion by frequently using the vernacular term "chesha" for the English word "ancestor worship." Except among those who became converts earliest in the history of the Christian church in this land, hardly anyone is to be found whose conscience can taboo chesha as a kind of idolatry. There is a great variety of inward attitudes taken by Christians toward this problem, while their outward attitudes remain identical as viewed by the outside public--that of tabooing it as a form of idolatry. Despite all the various shades of lenient views taken by individual Christians on this archrite of the people, in the eyes of the non-Christian public in general, we Christians appear to be irreconcilable iconoclasts, deadly enemies of the native culture, just because our better, fairer views, smothered and latent as they are, have not been crystallized and because the more enlightened attitude that the Christian churches as a body ought to take has not been declared and made known to them. I am sure that you would like to know just how things have developed so as to lead the Christians to draw themselves up and into alignment on the side of a gross and ungraceful, if not ungrateful, form of iconoclasm. To your supposed desire I will therefore address myself at once.

It is almost inherent in limited human nature that people will tend to doubt whether a truth that they have happened to receive in a set form of their own could possibly be conveyed in another form that has been so long holding the all-important Truth. Having held the truth for so long in this one form, it often seems impossible to them--or it has never occurred to them to try--to separate the form from the Truth it holds. All of us seem to be born purblind and need spectacles suitable for each of us in order to see things clearly as they really are. We are so sure that our own sight has been helped by the pair of spectacles that we have long been so used to that we often obstinately impose that very pair upon others; and we are no less often distressed at the fact that these wonderful eyeglasses--contrary to all expectation--do not work quite so perfect a miracle for others as they did for their original possessors. We sometimes willfully ignore the Truth when we encounter it enveloped in other forms than ours, as if we unconsciously feared that we would slacken our hold upon that dear form in which the Truth is encased--a better Truth, as we believe, owing to its "better" form, and in so doing lose sight of the Truth itself. God knows our limits; He forgives, nay, even smiles, I believe, at the small, nice prudence with which we are jealous for His great cause.

It is altogether fitting for ordinary Christians, who may never have happened to step out beyond the boundaries of their own dear community, to worship God quietly, undisturbed, and in the form so natural and so familiar to them. But what ought to be the stand of the great apostle of Christ, whose mission is to call men of all ranks and conditions from among the Gentiles, to live the perfect life of God's only begotten Son, the Christ? He finds himself suddenly surrounded by a people of different customs, different rites, different traditions. He feels himself deserted among an unfeeling multitude, who never seem to worry themselves about understanding his great message. He is somewhat in the same situation in which his Master was placed when He was on this earth. As his Master faced Hebrew laws, prophets, and traditions, he, too, encountered a different set of laws, sages, and hereditary customs. I wonder whether the first thing for him to do would not be to live and understand the things around him, to recognize the good that God has wrought in the people before him, and to continue the Father's work rather than initiate his own work, so as to help the people grow to the full stature of Jesus Christ, without violent, dangerous shocks.

I believe that those pioneer missionaries and others following them were all honest Christians, loving-hearted, helpful, blameless in conduct, unpolluted in heart. They were all right in themselves. They kept their own souls clean; and I do not doubt but that God has received some of them who are now dead into His everlasting glory. Nevertheless, I cannot readily admit that many real apostles of Christ have been sent to this land. To speak without restraint, I seriously doubt, in fact, that even a single man worthy of the name of apostle has ever been sent or come himself to this land. I know of no man of flaming vision who has come here, no man with a fiery passion for souls, in whose eyes the crucified and risen Lord is all in all, who defies every obstacle that stands in the way of reclaiming the lost soul to its life-giving God, and who masterfully and authoritatively promulgates, from inspiration and direct revelation from Christ (regardless of those apostles in Jerusalem) the new way of salvation for the people whose life it is his sacred trust to ennoble and amplify through Jesus Christ.

They kept their own society; they clung to their own forms of worship. They did not dare to think otherwise than that their own ways would do for the Korean converts exactly the same good that they had done for themselves. They never gave serious consideration to the things that had been taking place in Korea for thousands of years among the people to whom they came as perfectors, teachers. They believed that the light was on their side; so they thought that they did not need to consult the other side. They seem to have thought that God's work in the land began only when they landed on its shore. Wherefore, they seem to have asked, should they then regard its God-less past? With this kind of preconception that hurriedly glanced at strange phenomena that they had never seen before, they sincerely but hastily uttered adamantine judgments. Ancestor worship is one of the many things that were thus swept away in the avalanche of condemnation and have never been reconsidered with due proceedings.

The missionaries were quickly followed by mimicking Korean Christians, who took them as examples, even outdoing the missionaries' in the harshness of their verdicts. They banned chesha as an act of downright revolt against God. They made it a fundamental condition that a proselyte should forego this abomination first of all. Though it may be urged that this misjudgment was wholly ascribable to the early Korean Christians, missionaries are not entirely blameless inasmuch as they were their guides in the new faith and they ought to have guarded their weak brothers against the misapplication of the spirit of the new faith in regard to old things. The missionaries, hungry as they were to make their new comrade soldiers look like themselves in every particular, and impatient as they were to see their new brothers free from all seeming tinges of native superstition, were rather joyous at seeing them growing indifferent and cold to whatever smelled Korean just as they themselves felt naturally inclined to do.

I admit that there is still mimicry enough in this land for the old mode of evangelization to feed upon. But a Christian church should be ashamed to avail itself of such an ignoble inclination as mimicry. Every being, human or other, demands a fair deal and no more--he asks for square treatment. Harshness, intentional or unintentional, is as false an attitude as flattery. Let us be just and fair; only then will our cause prosper.

Now let us see whether ancestor worship in this land is really a form of idolatry. In the preceding section, five distinct features of idolatry were distinguished. Let us now go on to see whether chesha has all, or only some, of these features. The first feature of idolatry was held to be the fact that it is something beside God, therefore against God. The question is, "Is this also a feature of chesha?" "No!" is the answer; for it is quite contradictory to believe that God has given us a commandment, "Honor thy father and mother," and to hold at the same time that a certain embodiment of the spirit of this very law is something against God, however childish the manner of its expression may appear. Veneration for the memory of one's father and mother as practised in Korea can by no means constitute a sin against God, as there is good ground to believe that it is rather encouraged than forbidden by the spirit of the commandment. In the case of the Koreans, this commemoration is extended to their grandparents, great grandparents, and great great grandparents, whom the commemorators, in many cases, have never seen personally. You may say that the profuseness of the rite is pitifully ridiculous. Yes. But what of it? Profuseness does not change its quality. It is one thing to laugh at its ridiculous profusion, and it is another to slander its nature. Therefore, on the strength of the fact that we can honour the sweet memory not only of our fathers but also of our friends, and yet, with a conscience not a bit besmirched, can worship our God with whole-hearted devotion, I declare that so-called ancestor worship is no adversary of God. It is a superficial human judgment that has set it up against God.

Secondly, without being willfully unjust or even cruel, we cannot charge it with greed, which forms so conspicuous a feature in the case of idolatry. So far from actuated by this vulgar desire, the ancestor commemorators are so heedless of material loss in performing their filial duty that bankruptcy is often the result in the long run.

Thirdly, the motive is equally free of any form of fear, which was enumerated as the third feature of idolatry. Indeed, if the most ignorant among them have any superstitious fears to allay or greed to satisfy, they resort to other spirits or idols; they never appeal to their ancestors for protection or for prosperity. In connection with this time-honoured rite, there is no other association in their minds than that of filial duty. Indeed, most men, especially good scholars of the Confucian type, abhor the making of any appeal to any spirit or idol. It is mostly the female population that are subject to superstitious habits, to which they resort, in most cases, with stealthy avoidance of their husband's or grown-up-sons' knowledge.

Fourthly, it is so self-evident that I need not waste words to prove it that chesha is ethical, while any form of idolatry is unethical. Of course, it is not because chesha is a religious rite of the people that it is ethical, but because it deals with a relationship between ancestor and posterity--that is, between man and man.

Since these four features of idolatry cannot be identified in chesha, it is already too evident to need any further argument that it is untenable to classify the latter with the former. Notwithstanding these overwhelming proofs in favour of chesha, let us behave like a worthy judge and calmly hear the case to the last. The last feature specified as a characteristic of idolatry is the fact that it involves a deified object of vision. Some might exclaim: "You are there at last! What is the ancestral tablet, unless it is a kind of idol?" The one and only favour that I ask of such people is that they should do away with their prepossessions. Prepossessions always involve an expenditure of time and argument to lay them at rest.

An ancestral tablet is a tablet in the uncorrupted sense of the word-- a reminder with some inscription upon it. It is an oblong piece of wood with some such words:

Grandfather's (official station, if any) Noble
Spirit His Loyal Grandson (the name of the
family head)

Out of reverence, Koreans do not mention or read their father's names; and even those words of different construction, yet of the same pronunciation, are forbidden to be read. So it is quite obvious why they do not put down their fathers' names on the ancestral tablet, though they do record their official stations. In the case of a female ancestor, only her family name is permitted to be written. Indeed, women in this land, strictly speaking, had no names of their own, until very recently, except their family names.

The decorum of a respectable family requires that four successive lineal ancestors, counting back from the deceased parents (or one of them), of the head of the family should be commemorated. The normal number of persons thus held in commemoration was eight, though sometimes it could come to over twelve, second and third wives being taken into the reckoning. This being the case, I wonder whether one of the reasons for keeping tablets is not simply to remember so many persons. Among poor, illiterate classes, who cannot afford to provide such costly tablets, when occasions of memorial service come, they substitute scraps of paper for them, on which almost exactly the same words are put down. Most of these classes do not keep a recorded genealogy of their family, and their memorial services are usually confined to those by whose fond care they were brought up. If this single consideration were alone at issue, one might vote for illiteracy. It is always those ignoramuses, those children, that keep our manners primitive and give a new zest for life to our form-bound world. We need not doubt that the almost offensive excessiveness of the rite is only an overgrowth, stereotyped by a band of nitpicking Confucians. Long ago, there were laws providing that the number of ancestors memorialized should differ according to one's social status, emperors outdoing nobles; nobles, in their turn, outstripping plebians or common citizens in this special rite. No such distinctions enacted by law are now extant, except that the imperial family still clings to the old custom of commemorating five successive lineal ancestors.

With a little thought, we can well imagine--and it is the fact--that when the family head dies and his eldest son succeeds him, all of the ancestral tablets have to be scraped off and rewritten because the relations between the new head of the family and his ancestors are quite different from those between the deceased and them; and also that the earliest couple of ancestors have to be taken off from what may be called "commemoration list." These superannuated tablets, so to speak, are buried away.

All these facts being taken into consideration, we can hardly doubt that the ancestral tablet is in no manner an idol. It is neither an image nor a picture. It simply reminds us of the existence of our fathers' spirits. If the people handle them reverently, it is not because they believe that these wooden tablets are the spirits of their forefathers. How could they act differently while they show so much deference at the mere mention of their names? Strips of paper with inscriptions on them are widely used as substitutes for the wooden tablets, and it is only to our own discredit that we perversely go so far as to say that these poor Koreans take these miserable pieces of paper to be their fathers' spirits and then throw them into the fire the instant the occasion is over.

For the sake of argument, let me concede to my supposed opponent's view that some Koreans do seriously take the ancestral tablets to be their fathers' very spirits. Then what of that? There is a certain amount of stupidity in all of this, and nothing more. So long as they do honour to their fathers' names, it does not materially change the real meaning of the rite. And we must frankly admit that there was as much, if not more, studpidity in the old Jewish custom of offering multivarious kinds of sacrifices to God. "Pshaw! You talk out of place," you might say; "that Jewish law, you must remember, symbolically represents a truth that is so dear to us." Yes, I myself do not want to be outdone in recognizing the eternal Truth in the Jewish ritual, whose purifying presence emanates through its rough husk as a beautiful person radiates despite his shabby garment--nay, a Truth that has sanctified the little stupidity around it and even seems to have changed the guileless foolishness into a wisdom of everlasting salvation. But, for all this, some stupidity there was. By this I do not mean to apologize for the atmosphere of foolishness that envelopes this particular custom. What I mean is simply this: Foolishness is no sin, if it only be sincere; it may be an effect of accumulated sins, but can never be sin itself. This statement can be defied only when we are so rash as to confound punishment with crime, effect with cause.

In the light, however weak it may be, of the foregoing argument that ancestor worship has no kindred feature whatever with any of the five characteristics of idolatry, it may safely be concluded that the charge of idolatry is anything but just.

Chapter V

Ancestor Worship: From the Perspective of Modernization

Bong-ho Son

<u>Opening remarks</u>

The history of the practice of ancestor worship in Korea is characterized by much shedding of blood. When Roman Catholicism was introduced to Korea in the beginning of the 17th century through Korean scholars, fierce conflicts erupted between the conservative Neo-Confucian scholars and the progressive Roman Catholic converts and their sympathizers over the matter of ancestor worship. Interlocked with political factional fighting, the Roman Catholic refusal of the rites resulted in the execution of more than ten thousand persons during the following three centuries. Perhaps no nation has produced so many martyrs over the issue of ancestor worship. Protestantism, however, which was introduced much later toward the end of the 19th century, met with much less opposition mainly because by then the Neo-Confucian dynasty had lost its control over society. Even though official persecution was less, personal hostility remained strong until recent days; and even today it has not entirely disappeared. Ironically, Roman Catholics in Korea today have a much more compromising attitude toward the rites than do Protestants.

The bloody struggles over the practices involved in ancestor worship have to a large extent been relegated in today's Korea to a chapter in its history. Ancestor worship is no longer as eagerly and widely practiced as it once was. A rough survey among university students[1] shows that about a half of all Korean families do not practice it. Considering that around one-quarter of the Korean population is Christian, we can safely assume that about one-third of Korean nonbelievers does not observe the ancestral rites. It is true that some Christians still practice it, but the number is negligible and decreasing. In spite of the recent resurgence of interest in traditional cultures among the people of the Third

World, various factors indicate that ancestor worship in Korea will not be revived very strongly.

In the following pages an analysis will be made of changes in the attitudes of Koreans toward their ancestral rites. This study may assist Korean Christians in determining their future course so as to speed up the change; and it may aid Christian Chinese and Japanese brothers in meeting the challenges in their own respective societies more effectively. The basic question here posed, then, is "What factors have contributed to the change of attitude toward the practice of ancestor worship in Korea?"

Weakened status of Confucianism

The rites of ancestor worship, though found in many places including Africa and practiced also in pre-Confucian China, are generally associated with Confucianism. Especially in Korea, the rites were introduced from China toward the end of the 13th century along with Neo-Confucianism. And they were encouraged and even enforced by the government throughout the Rhee Dynasty (1392-1910), which adopted Neo-Confucianism as its official ideology.

One can legitimately question whether Confucianism is a religion; but one cannot question the fact that it has exercised as much cultural influence upon Korea as any religion could. During the last 500 years before the Japanese occupation, Confucianism controlled almost all sectors of Korean life. Thus, it has made a lasting impact upon Korean culture and its ways of thinking. Along with China and Japan, Korea is rightly classified as a Confucian nation.

The position that Confucianism occupies in modern Korea, however, has been weakened ever since the fall of the Yi Dynasty. Several factors have been decisive in this decline.

Unlike Buddhism and Christianity, Confucianism has no official institutions to serve as the carriers of its teachings and transmitters of its traditions. Once the political authority that has supported it is removed, Confucianism is left with no centers to preserve its identity. This is perhaps one of the reasons why Confucianism is not regarded as a religion by most Koreans. In spite of the fact that in many respects the Korean mentality remains strongly Confucian, few Koreans regard themselves as

Confucians; and in official statistical tables Confucianism is being deleted from the list of major religions.

Another important reason for the weakening of Confucian influences in Korea may be its Chinese origin. No Korean would deny his cultural indebtedness to China; but few are proud of it. When the country was occupied by the Japanese, many thinking Koreans put the blame for this tragedy upon the political factional fighting that prevailed during the 18th century when there was much contention among Confucian scholars about trivial matters such as ancestral rites. These struggles were cited as the main cause of national demoralization. As a result, an unusual proportion of nationalist leaders were converted to Christianity. Seung Man Rhee, the first president of the Republic, was one of them. Even today, Korean historians pay special attention to the Sil-Hak (Real Learning) scholars of the 18th century, who were mainly Roman Catholic believers, or to those who were inspired by them. These scholars were very critical of the Neo-Confucianism that was then dominant. Both the fact that the Real Learning scholars could be critical of the Dynasty's offical ideology and that modern historians evaluate these scholars positively reflect a nationalistic sentiment. The situation might have been quite different if Neo-Confucianism were of Korean origin.

The Chinese origin of Confucianism and of the ancestral rites provides Korean Christians with an easy counter-argument when they are challenged about neglecting indigenous traditions. If Korean culture has been determined by Buddhism and Confucianism, both of which are of foreign origin, Christians can answer that there is no reason why Christianity cannot take a part. This rationale can be applied in particular against the ancestral rites. Although few Christians really make use of this weapon and few Koreans are always conscious of it, the fact is there; and Koreans can be very easily made conscious of this reasoning. Whenever foreign religions are at issue, this argument can be effectively used.

Secularization of the traditional world view

One of the most important causes for the change of attitude toward ancestor worship in Korea is the general trend of cultural secularization. The traditional picture of the universe is no longer accepted by modern

Koreans, who have received an education oriented toward the world view of the secular sciences. Undoubtedly, the practice of ancestor worship is rooted in an outdated world view; and any replacement of this anachronistic outlook would necessarily affect ancestor worship. Even though few Koreans are aware of the relationship between the two, the incongruity of ancestor worship with a secular world view can be easily seen. Customs and habits upon which people do not reflect may last for centuries, but they are also very weak when challenged.

Of the many aspects of the traditional world view that are undergoing transformation, two are most relevant to the present discussion. Examining them, one may see how the secularization of culture necessarily affects the practice of ancestor worship.

A. Past-oriented view of time

The Confucian view of time, like most traditional views, is clearly past oriented. Van Groningen, in his study of Greek thinking, says of the Greek mind:

> His longing is a longing back. Plato assures us that the Ancients were better than we ourselves and lived in closer communion with Gods. Socrates places everything which he thinks desirable in the past; the Athens of former days was exemplary; only imitation of the forefathers can bring real prosperity; as with Homer "the strength of Hercules" is a natural paraphrase of the simple name, so with him "the excellency of fathers" becomes a synonym of the fathers themselves.[2]

We can say almost the same of the Confucian mind. The "Ideal Model" of all human history existed in the past in the days of Yao and Shun or of the Three Emperors. The subsequent endeavors of all of humanity are directed to the approximation of the virtues of the past, since no one could really improve upon those virtues. This preference for the old is reflected in the general Confucian emphasis on history, genealogy, and ancestor worship. Chen-shu is quoted approvingly by Chu-hsi, the founder of Neo-Confucianism, as lamenting: "In ancient times young people followed their elders but now elders follow young people because they do not know their origin."[3] He relates the past-oriented view of time to the honoring of their forefathers. Past practice is preferred, and the reason for the preference is that young people follow their elders. Van Groningen also relates the Greek cult of ancestors and heroes with the past-oriented view of time espoused by the Greeks.

The worship of dead ancestors, filial duties to parents, and the honoring of one's elders were apparently much more than simply ethical requirements. The Chinese most likely thought that because ancestors, parents, and elders lived closer in time to the ideal ages, they were in fact better than themselves and worthy of true respect.

Francis Bacon, a major British philosopher of the 17th century, surprised his contemporaries with the matter-of-fact statement that "We know more than the ancients." The fact that this statement came as a surprise suggests that a similar frame of mind can be expected to prevail among all peoples who hold to a past-oriented view of time. Even Confucius never dared to suggest that he was better than the ancients nor that he said anything really new that the ancient sages had not already advanced. Creativity was almost blasphemy. The high regard for the past is eloquently represented by the interesting historical fact that the Korean alphabet, which is the most scientific of all alphabets, and the easiest to learn and use, was buried unused for about 400 years. The Korean alphabet was unused, even though it was invented by the King, simply because it was new and different from the traditional Chinese characters.

Modern secularized people on the other hand, are not willing to accept the past without question. In spite of a reviving interest of young Koreans in the past, few sincerely believe that the ancients knew better and were in fact better than themselves. Creativity and new knowledge in science and technology are more highly valued today than anything else, and the past-oriented view of time has no place now except for those who have failed to cope with the new developments.

Trivial as it may be, the change of temporal outlook is reflected in the uses of calendar and "year tellings." The names of the months of the year based upon the zodiac, a remnant of the circular and past-oriented view of time and once very popular, are no longer used in Korea except during the first few days of the new year, or by fortunetellers. "Year tellings" in official documents and history books follow the Western system of A.D. and B.C., which is based upon a linear philosophy of time. Neither are the first and the 15th days of the month especially marked by Koreans.

Within this changed cultural setting the ancestral rites have lost the support from the past-oriented view. Such ancestral practices will grow increasingly out of date as the forward-looking young generation replaces the old. Thus, the rejection of ancestor worship is becoming a kind of etiquette without binding force.

    B. A naturalistic world view

The past-oriented view of time is an aspect of the naturalistic world view held by most ancient cultures. Confucianism is also basically naturalistic, even though to a lesser degree than Taoism. According to this view, nature is not only the organic whole of what exists but is also the norm that everyone must follow. To act counter to nature is not only impossible but also immoral and inhuman. The Five Principles of Confucian ethics are supposedly all based upon intrinsic human nature, which is an integral part of the whole of nature--that is, of all of heaven and earth. The Empire is a microcosm, the family a smaller microcosm; and individuals are the smallest microcosm of all. Respect for the head of the house and ultimately for the Emperor is, therefore, concommitant with respect for the total universe or the natural order. Thus, the practice of ancestor worship is rooted in naturalism. "Furthermore, it is according to the Principle of Nature that there should be a system of the head of descent. It is like a tree. There must be the main trunk which shoots straight up from the root, and there must also be branches."[5] "The Principle of showing gratitude to one's ancestors through sacrifical rites is rooted in the human mind. Sages instituted the rites merely to bring virtues to perfection. Even the wolf and the otter can perform sacrifical rites."[6] Negligence of ancestor worship is, therefore, the ignoring of what is natural to human beings and is therefore sacrilegious. It incurs nature's terrible revenge upon oneself and one's community.

The idea of sacred nature is, however, no longer accepted today. As the pressures to industrialize mount, economically backward Korea has been forced to exploit her relatively meager natural resources as much as possible; and this exploitation has inevitably altered people's traditional reverence for nature. Of course, economic pressure is not the only factor behind the secularization of nature. Modern scientific education, cultural contacts with the West, and the growth of Christian influence have all contributed to this secularization. Koreans now exploit nature so fearlessly that we must worry about environmental pollution. Nature needs to be protected instead of being worshiped and obeyed. She has lost her sacred allure and is no longer feared. Fear of nautre's revenge upon those who disobey her taboos has lost its power. Moreover, few people really believe any longer that worshiping dead ancestors is as natural to people as it has been taught to be. Most people who practice it do so because of custom or habit. They do not regard such worship as a moral obligation. Thus, ancestor worship has lost its metaphysical and religious support in Korea.

Disintegration of traditional family and social structures

The practice of ancestor worship is integrated and encouraged by certain types of social and family structures. At the beginning, only prominent figures and emperors were allowed to be worshiped after their death, not only in China but also in Korea. Gradually, however, the ancestors of prominent families were also allowed to be so honored. Cheng-Shu says:

Since there are no heads of descent today, there are no ministers at court who have come from families noted for generations. The system of heads of descent is in place, people can then know how to honor their ancestors and can take their origins seriously. As they take their origins seriously the power of the court will naturally be highly respected... Only when there is a distinction between the superior and the inferior, between the high and low, can there be obedience without disorder. How can this be achieved without a system by which to know where people belong?[7]

When the offspring of prominent figures enjoyed special privileges and honors in a class society and only they were allowed to offer sacrifices to their ancestors, it was natural that the rites themselves would be regarded as something honorable. When Neo-Confucianism was introduced to Korea in the 13th century, the ancestral rites were also used as a means of educating people to be virtuous. At first, only prominent scholars and benevolent officals were given the privilege of being worshiped after their death. But by the 14th century the government extended the practice to common people as well. Lower-class people must have thought it a great privilege, since their ancestors were then treated equally with the notables. The practice had ulterior motives, however, besides that of pure love for one's ancestors. Ancestors were worshiped not only for the sake of the dead but also, and perhaps more, for that of the living. In fact, the latter motive is predominant in today's practice.

Such a social practice is neither tenable nor desirable today. Fortunately, family lineage is not considered very important now, except in the selecting of spouses. Good education and excellent character are counted more than good breeding. Usually only the less-educated people adhere to the traditions of ancestor worship in Korea today.

Family lineage and the ancestral rites have also lost their importance because the extended-family system is disappearing. Owing to increasing social mobility, the size of the family has grown smaller, and brothers and cousins are scattered in different places. This makes family gatherings for ancestral rites increasingly difficult and seldom observed. Young cousins brought up in different places do not feel any strong kinship. Traditionally, first sons were given the obligation of preparing the ceremony. But its significance is being obscured as parents usually stay in the countryside while young couples move to cities and as the number of families with only one son multiply due to family planning. Nor is the traditional authority of the elder brother any longer much respected. All of these changes work against continuing the ancestral rites.

Sense of estrangement toward the rites

Another factor, which seems rather trivial but forms, nevertheless, an important obstacle to continuing the practice, is the growing sense of enstrangement toward certain elements of the ancestral rites. Perhaps this may be a symptom rather than a cause of the decline of Confucianism and the rites.

An example of these elements is the tablets that are placed upon the altar of ancestral sacrifice. They are supposed to summon the spirits of the ancestors for whom the sacrifice is made. The tablets, however, are always written in Chinese and the contents vary according to the sex, offical status, and the distance in the genealogy of the ancestor concerned. Also, the material used and the way it is folded are all strictly formalized.

Most young Koreans, however, are not very familiar with all these rituals. The Chinese words on the tablets and their composition are so unusual that they mean almost nothing to most Koreans. Not many young Koreans would know how to fold the tablets and even fewer know how to properly write the appropriate words on them. Strangely enough, no Korean would dare to write Korean words on them. (Just as the Danish sentinel in Shakespeare's Hamlet believed that ghosts could only understand Latin, Koreans believe unconsciously that even Korean ghosts can only understand Chinese.)

The use of Chinese contrasts clearly with shamanism. Shamanism is the oldest living cult in the Korean peninsula and is still active in rural areas and city slums. The shaman's chants of invocation have always employed the language of the common people, and they are very flexible in incorporating any new elements. Modern shamans, for instance, name the ghosts of victims of traffic accidents in their invocations. It is to the disadvantage of the ancestral rites that they are not as flexible as shamanism.

Besides the tablets, the arrangement of food on the offering table poses another problem. The food must be arranged in a particular order, but few young Koreans have learned the order or bother to learn it. The long-legged altar tables are a nuisance for families that have to move quite often. And the incense burners used at the rites are out of harmony with the Western style of furniture used in ultramodern apartments.

All of these factors, though seemingly unimportant, create a psychological distance from the rites and work negatively against them unless a strong motivation for continuing the rites is provided.

Christian influence on society

 Another strong force behind the decline of the practice of ancestor worship in Korea is undoubtedly the Christian influence on the society. Statistically, Christians count as a quarter of the total population; but on certain issues such as ancestral practices, their influence is greater than their number might suggest. The majority of Protestant Christians are convinced opponents of the practice, and this opposition is felt in society through various avenues. Christians involved in education, policy making, journalism, and other fields would not eagerly encourage, enforce, or even draw attention to ancestor worship. Together, they create a social atmosphere that is not favorable to the continuation of the tradition.

 This climate of opinion against ancestor worship is enhanced by the fact that there are proportionally more Christians among the educated than among the uneducated classes. This fact also effectively counters the old accusation that those who neglect the rites are ignorant and bestial.

Concluding remarks

 The only religious element in Confucianism, the practice of ancestor worship, is on the verge of extinction in Korea, for it has been unable to accommodate the new environment or to force society to accommodate its demands. Even if the habitual practices should be continued for some time, they are now deprived of their religious contents. Whether Korean Christians should object to the ancestral rites in this diluted form has to be carefully studied. The Apostle Paul's teachings in the Eighth Chapter of I Corinthians may be relevant to this question.

 Korean Christians should also be wary of overkill. Their fight against traditionalism and ancestor worship should not imply an unconditional Westernization nor discard the good aspects of the tradition. The worship of money and possessions is not a superior alternative to idolatrous ancestor worship. The valuable tradition of obedience to parents and respect for elders must by all means be kept alive. Thus, ancestor worship should be examined not only in terms of the Second Commandment but also in terms of the Fifth.

Notes

[1]This survey was made by the writer at the beginning of April, 1983, in three different classes at Seoul National University and Hankuk University of Foreign Studies, both of which are secular institutions.

[2]B.A. Van Groningen, In the Grip of the Past: Essay on an Aspect of Greek Thought (Leiden, Brill, 1953), p. 7.

[3]Chu Hsi and Lu Tsu-chien compiled, Reflections on Things at Hand: The Neo-Confucian Anthology (tr. Wing-Tsit Chan), (New York: Columbia University Press, 1967), pp. 232-33.

[4]Ibid., pp. 82-83.

[5]Chu Hsi ans Lu, op. cit., p. 232.

[6]Ibid., p. 226.

[7]Ibid., pp. 231-32.

Chapter VI

Ancestor Worship: From the Perspective of Family Life

Wi Jo Kang

"Ancestor worship is the origin of all religions." If we support this statement made in 1855 by Herbert Spencer, we can also say that ancestor worship is the foundation of all culture, for the cultures of nations are rooted in religions. As Paul Tillich said, "Religions are the essence of human cultures and cultures are the forms of religions."

In fact, the practice of ancestor worship in Korea can be traced back to the beginning of its history. The mythology of Tangun, the foundation myth of Korea, is a good example of a remembered ancestral origin of the Korean people. Whatever the historical factuality of the mythology may be, it is nonetheless true that throughout the history of Korea the Korean people have remembered their national ancestor Tankun and worshiped him just as individual families have also remembered their own ancestors on holidays and on the anniversaries of their deaths with offerings of food, incense, and prayers. Besides, because of Korea's geographical proximity to China, Confucian culture, which emphasized family life and filial piety, was also strongly influencial in the formulation of Korean cultural characteristics. In Confucian society the family is the center of all things and the family determines the values, personal ethics, and norms of social behavior. The center or basic foundation of family is, in turn, the filial piety of the descendents toward their ancestors expressed in their offering of sacrifices to the ancestral spirits. A filial piety that included faithful remembrance of the ancestors and the legacy of the family was considered the highest form of filial piety and the root of all virtues. As one Confucian sage said: "Filial piety is the way of Heaven, the principle of earth, and the practical duty of man."[1] Chinese virtues and values are always understood within the context of filial piety, and the highest degree of filial piety is always associated with ancestor worship. Through ancestor worship, the children remember and nourish the wills of their parents through whom the children had the source of their lives. Thereby, the parents achieve immortality and the unfinished tasks of the ancestors' lives are carried out by the family's descendents.

Under the strong impetus of these Confucian teachings on filial piety, the Korean people institutionalized ancestor worship as a basic affair of the family. One anthropologist rightly concludes:

> In societies in which religious worship is basically a family affair, strong interrelationships between family organization and religious structure exist. In these societies, the household religion is generally ancestor worship.[2]

After the 14th century, when the Yi Dynasty was established, Neo-Confucianism, which still strongly emphasized filial piety and the practice of ancestor worship, became a national institution for all Koreans. No one in any segment of Korean society who wished to be accepted as a legitimate and respectful member of that society could escape practicing ancestor worship. The Yi government built many Confucian schools throughout the country and continued to teach the virtues of filial piety and the proper rites of ancestor worship. Confucian temples were also built beside the schools in important towns throughout the country, and pictures of Confucian sages were placed in them and worshiped with elaborate ceremonies and sacrifical offerings.

After the fashion of the Confucian temples, individual clans and families also faithfully observed the rites of ancestor worship; and the long rule of the Yi family was maintained from the 14th century into the early 20th century by the strong integrating influence of ancestor worship in Korean society as a whole.

Thus, ancestor worhsip became a powerful institution in Korean life and culture. It was a sacred symbol in which all Koreans found meaning and purpose for their lives and the enhancement of their sense of belonging. Without both ancestor worship and family, Koreans lost the sense of meaning of their existence; but through the observance of these rites Koreans maintained the values of filial piety and loyalty, which in turn strengthened family life and solidified the fabric of Korean society.

The reenactment of living memories in the rites of ancestor worship should not be prohibited, but should be preserved in the Christian family as well. It is, after all, a Biblical imperative to remember one's ancestors and respect one's family lineage. It is God's will that Christians should remember their ancestors and honor them, as Koreans have been doing for centuries. The Korean Christian family should not be separated from this time-honored practice, but should continue to use it to strengthen family life and provide good examples of filial piety.

The question remains, however, how a Christian family can observe such rites in honor of its ancestors. In answer to this query, I propose the practice of Eucharistic services in the Christian home. For a great many people the Christian life is confined within the church structure and centered around a monologue by the preacher-priest. However important this may be, Christian life is more than activities within a church building focusing upon a pastoral office. Indeed, Christian life suffers if the nurture of the followers of our Lord by Word and Sacrament is the prerogative only of the clergy and occurs only within the church building. Surely, the doctrine of the priesthood of all believers must be evident in all phases of the Christian life. This pervasiveness can enable the laity to participate fully in the appreciation of God's gifts, including the administration of the Lord's Supper in their own homes. This is not to deny the importance of the office of the ordained ministry and the role of the preacher-priest in nurturing Christian life. But the concern raised by Korean Christians demands a response; it provides us with the opportunity to ask ourselves, "How can the Church incorporate the laity into its ministry in a meaningful way?" In furthering this end, it will be necessary to decentralize Christian life, moving it away from the confinement to a church building and to the hands of a preacher-priest, and thus to initiate a new Christian sacramental life predicated upon the active participation and leadership of the laity within the structure of family life. It is important for families to encounter the life-giving Sacrament and Word in their homes, under the leadership of the parents.

God's design for people is that they should live within family structures. All of the activities of life, including any worship centered in the church building, should complement this family life. Indeed, the metaphor of family life is used in Scripture to describe the intimacy of fellowship in the Christian community. The important lesson we learn from Scripture is that of centering daily life around the Christ. If the imagery of the people of God as one family under God is to become meaningful in congregational life, then the Chruch must assist each individual family in constructing a strong identity in its family life. This can and should be developed through Word and Sacrament in the context of family life within the home as part of the responsibility of family members.

However, traditional church life has not provided opportunities or support for the active participation of the laity in nurturing, strenghtening, and preserving true Christian faith within the family. Some Christians tend to separate religious life from daily life, viewing their homes as secular, or even profane, institutions while the Church is the only sacred institution in the human community. Many Christians today are unable to see the manifestations of the sacred within family life and may even view any administration of the Sacrament in the home as sacrilegious.

However, this denial of the use of the means of grace in the home is a major factor contributing to the view of the home as profane. Allowing home administration of the Lord's Supper would be one means of overcoming this misunderstanding and enriching Christian family life. I am proposing that the head of the family administer the Lord's Supper at home for special occasions of family celebration and family need, just as the Jewish celebration of the Passover is presided over by the head of the family. The Passover was instituted within the context of family life and has continually been celebrated within that same context down to the present day. Whether the Last Supper was or was not a Passover meal is an academic question; certainly, the Eucharist that Christ instituted is more than some type of continuation of the Passover. The Christian faith, while acknowledgeing its roots in the heritage of Jewish faith, does not base its liturgical practices on the details and particulars of Jewish custom. Nonetheless, it is questionable whether it is essential that the celebration of the Lord's Supper be entirely separated from the life of the individual family; and it is doubtful whether participation should be so delimited that even the head of the family has no responsibility other than his passive reception at the alter rail within the church building, where the administration of the Sacraments remains in the hands of the preacher-priest.

The role of "head of the family" can be seen as an important part in our understanding and practice of the family Eucharist. It is important to remember that in its very origin the Christian Church was associated with worship among families within the homes of the first Christians. This origin creates an opportunity for the Christian Church to incorporate the laity into the ministry of the Church by drawing upon the rich heritage of family life and by practicing meaningful worship in the home including the duty to offer there the Sacrament of the Altar and to "remember the days of old, consider the years of many generations..." (Deut. 32:7). There is the promising possibility that to allow the celebration of the Eucharist in the home will more firmly establish the role of the head of the family. This would not be some type of glorious elevation of the family head, nor a usurping of the prerogatives of the preacher-priest; but it would be an occasion for strengthening the bonds of family life and for appreciating the family heritage and the life of its forebears.

Within such a scheme the person who is responsible for the family, whether a woman or a man, can take seriously the duties and obligations of presiding over the reading of the Word and celebrating the Eucharist, and can do so on the date of an ancestor's death according to Confucian custom. The person responsible for the service would have some members of the family read from Scripture and perhaps make a few relevant comments. Then, the presiding person would prepare the pastry or bread and native wine, consecrate them with the Words of Institution, and distribute the elements to all members of the family (excluding infants) with the words, "This is the body of Christ, given for you, as you remember your father's death." The blessing could be changed to fit the occasion. By receiving the elements they would be asking God to preserve and strengthen their faith unto life everlasting, in unity with the deceased members of the family.

What compelling reason forbids that this means of grace be brought within the home to strengthen Christian family life? There is nothing in the

Holy Scriptures that provides a theological basis for denying the consecration and administration of the Sacrament by the laity. The validity of the Sacrament depends neither upon theological education nor ordination. And, in fact, the Donatist heresy, which taught the opposite, was repeatedly condemned by the Church. It is Christ himself who is present in and provides the benefits of his life-giving meal in the form of bread and wine and this means of grace should be widely used in family life in reverence and remembrance of the ancestors.

Such administration of the Lord's Supper does contain, however, one dangerous element. The family might come to identify so strongly with their own personal celebration of the Communion that they could become separated from true fellowship in the broader Christian family that exists beyond the borders of family, nation race, and culture. But it does not, in fact, seem likely that a Christian who cherishes the body and blood of the Lord Jesus Christ in the home would in some way become alienated from the universal community that lives in Christ's presence. The family celebration of the Sacrament should never be regarded as the private property of any family, nor as sanctioning a departure from inclusive membership in the local church body. Rather, the purpose of "the Eucharist at home" must be to strengthen the Christian family everywhere, thereby rendering corporate worship more meaningful. The "Eucharist at Home" is a call to a renewed Christian faith through enriched Christian family life and may be a means for the emergence of a ministerial role for the laity.

This proposal for a "Eucharist at Home" is prompted by the sight of many Oriental Christian families who feel that their religious life is breaking away from its family-centered roots. Likewise, there is a destruction and weakening of the Christian family in Western society. In Oriental societies, especially in the Confucian-oriented societies of East Asia, all aspects of life center upon the family. The understanding of the universe, of the world, and even of the state are qualified by interpretation within the context of the family. When one becomes a Christian, this emphasis upon the family is diminished; and many Asian Christians feel the loss in their lives. Family devotions and prayer are all-important in a Christian family;

but one might ask "why not have even more devotional life in the family?" Here, an Oriental Christian would answer positively, stressing the importance of such devotional life. At the same time, however, the Oriental Christian would also ask, "Why not strengthen family devotional life by the administration of the Sacrament of the Altar within the family and by the head of the family and do so especially upon occasions of remembering the ancestors of the family?"

81

Notes

[1]Fung Yu-lan, A History of Chinese Philosophy (Princeton, N.J.: Princeton University Press, 1952), I, p. 359.

[2]Annemarie D. W. Malefijt, Religion and Cuture (New York: The Macmillan Co., 1968), p. 291.

[3]Allen D. Clark, A History of the Church in Korea (Seoul: The Christian Literature Society of Korea, 1971), p. 44.

[4]Hyobom B. Pak, China and the West: Myths and Realities in History (Leiden, The Netherlands: E.J. Brill, 1974), p. 87.

[5]C. K. Yang, Religion in Chinese Society (Berkeley, Calif.: University of California Press, 1970), p. 48.

[6]Pak, op. cit., p. 86.

Chapter VII

Ancestor Worship: From a Theological Perspective

Jung Young Lee

The Controversy over the practice of ancestor worship culminates as an issue in theology. And it would seem that the crux of all theological arguments is to be found in the notion of idolatry. Behind the theological issue, however, lies a cultural problem. Since no theological issue can be considered in isolation from its cultural context, we must deal with the cultural issue as a part of the theological problem.

Let us begin our discussion with the notion of idolatry, which for Christians has been the main obstacle to the practice of ancestor worship. At the outset it should be pointed out that it is almost axiomatic that idol worship should not be allowed by any Christian. Idol worship is contrary to the first and second commandments of God, which are conceived as the cornerstones of the Judeo-Christian idea of monotheism. No sound theology can take these commandments lightly.

To recall the first and second commandments of God, let us look at the passage in Exodus 20:3,4:

> You shall have no other gods before me. You shall not make yourself a graven image, or any likeness of any thing that is heaven above, or that is... You shall not bow down to them or serve them... but [shall] show steadfast love to thousands of those who love me and keep my commandments.

Most people who oppose the practice of ancestor worship uphold these two commandments as guidelines for the Judeo-Christian faith. Within this context, worshiping any gods or divine beings other than the God of Abraham, Isaac, and Moses is idolatry.

The idea of an idol is to be defined then in relation to worship. In other words, an idol is an object of worship. It is more than an image of the divine. An image in itself is not an idol in any strict sense. The image becomes an idol when it is made into an object of worship. Thus, the statues of Greek or Roman gods, Sam-sim or Mountain gods, and the like become idols only when they are worshiped. Likewise, the ancestral tablet or picture itself is not an idol. It can become an idol when it is worshiped. The first commandment, that "you should not have any gods before me," does not imply the denial of all other gods than the true God whom we worship. Rather, it seems to imply that if any other gods exist, none of them should take the place of God nor should they be placed before Him. In other words, we have been asked to worship God alone. Thus, the first commandment itself allows the possible existence of other gods besides Jehovah, though the latter takes priority above all others. So the monotheism of the Decalogue (or, speaking more strictly, its "monolatry") does not deny the existence of other gods, but demands our exclusive loyalty and devotion to the single God. This is why it is not possible to define idolatry without reference to our attitude toward the image that represents the divine. Worship and idolatry are then inseparable.

Before we examine the idea of worship, let us consider whether the ancestral tablet is capable of becoming an idol. As you may have noticed in the previous chapters of this book, those who are speculative and have received modern education tend to think that the ancestral tablet is none other than an image or a symbol that recalls the dead ancestor. Thus, in their view the ancestral tablet becomes a memorial. As such, it cannot be an idol. It may well be compared to a picture of the deceased that reminds us of the dead. Surely, having a picture of the dead cannot be considered as practicing idolatry. Likewise, to have the ancestral tablet at home is similar to hanging a picture of the dead ancestor on the wall. Therefore, those who think that the ancestral tablet merely recalls to our minds the dead ancestor can regard ancestor worship simply as a memorial service. Thus, we have no theological problem nor any need to deal with the issue of idolatry as long as ancestor worship is regarded as a memorial service.

There are many people, however, who still share the traditional belief that the dead soul resides not only in the burial site but in the ancestral tablet as well. They take the tablet seriously. Our special attention should therefore be paid to these people and their particular version of ancestor worship, because they not only comprise the majority of the Korean people but also create a serious problem for Christianity. These people usually belong to a lower social class and are less speculative. They are often called Minjung, the mass people.

If the dead soul resides in the tablet, then is the tablet an idol? First of all, let us make a distinction between the dead soul as residing in the tablet and the dead soul as identified with the tablet. However ignorant and uneducated the Korean worshiper might be, he knows that the tablet itself is not the dead soul. Everyone knows that upon the tablet the name of the dead is written by a man. It cannot, therefore, be identified with the dead soul. The dead soul can reside in the tablet, but not be identified with it. If the dead soul resides in the tablet, however, then the tablet is the image by which the presence of the ancestral soul is known to us. Since the tablet is an image that possesses the dead spirit, it is certainly capable of becoming an idol if the ancestral spirit or soul is considered divine. The question then becomes, "What is the nature of the dead soul?" And it is this question that determines whether the tablet is capable of becoming an idol. If the dead soul is the divine, the tablet that possesses the ancestral spirit can then qualify as an idol. Unless the dead soul is divine or possesses the divine quality, the ancestral tablet cannot become an idol. For example, a tree that contains energy cannot qualify as an idol; but a tree that contains the divine being is certainly so qualified. The kind of object that is qualified to be an idol must be regarded as divine and capable of replacing the real God or of becoming a hindrance to the worship of the highest God (Eph. 5:5; Phil. 3:19; John 5:20-21).

Is the dead soul a god or in any sense divine? Or is it hindrance to the worship of God? Let us deal with the former question first. The dead soul who resides in the ancestral tablet is regarded as a member of the family, possessing all human qualities other than physical presence. The dead soul has both advantages and disadvantages: his disadvantage is that he has to depend on the living, while his advantage is that he is capable of doing things that a living being cannot do. The dead soul needs to be cared for and fed by the living. On the other hand, the dead soul is powerful; for he has no physical limitations. The dead soul is powerful enough to bestow blessings upon the living or to cause them misfortune.

In this respect, both the dead and the living are mutually supportive and interdependent. But one who has to depend upon the living members of the family can hardly be called divine.

On the other hand, the ancestral soul or the dead soul is capable of becoming a divine being. In East Asian countries, the highest god has its origin in the ancestoral soul. The Shang-ti or the highest god in China, Whang-un or the highest god in Korea, and the Sungodess or the highest god in Japan are all regarded as the first ancestors of these people. Moreover, many great heroes and kings in Asia have been elevated to a divine status. The ancestral souls, therefore, are capable of becoming gods.

If the dead soul resides in the ancestral tablet and if he is capable of becoming a divine being, we can conclude that the ancestral tablet can become an idol and that ancestor worship can become idolatry. Although the tablet is capable of becoming an idol, it cannot be an idol unless it is worshiped. Thus, we must examine the notion of worship that the Korean people have in mind.

Various elements are included in the act of worship. One of the aspects most offensive to the Western missionaries and to which they have strongly objected is the act of bowing down before the ancestral tablet. Bowing down before a graven image is one of the clearest expressions of idolatry to the minds of Western missionaries. However, when it is observed from the perspective of the Korean culture, bowing down is an act of respect. Children bow down before their parents on special occasions, such as at birthday celebrations or at the new year festivities. They bow down to their living parents, and just so their parents bow down to the ancestral tablets. The act of bowing down can be seen as an expression of filial piety. In this respect, it is not unique to ancestor worship.

Let us now look at the offering placed upon the altar during ancestor worship. The offerings, which include such things as a cup of wine, fruit, and rice cakes, are identical with the ordinary foods offered to the living parents at special occasions. Traditionally, the father or grandfather had been given a special table at his meal. This same kind of table is also used when the food offerings are made to the ancestral tablet. The Korean people, like the Chinese, have a tendency to treat the dead as if they were living. Thus, the dead soul is given the same things that the living would receive. In this respect, the act of ancestor worship is an extension of ordinary life.

The pattern of Korean life here involved can be characterized simply as the accepted acts of prostration that convey respect for the elders and of offerings made to them with thanksgiving. These kinds of life patterns are employed, by extension, to the dead ancestors as well. In a way, ancestor worship is then the extension of living relations to the dead ancestors. Since the Korean people have been taught to treat the dead as if they were living, their dealings with a dead ancestor are not really different from those with a living father. Thus, it is difficult to construe ancestor worship as idolatry.

There is also another aspect of ancestor worship that we have not discussed so far. That is the frightfulness and power that have been associated with the spiritual beings when the ancestral rite is performed. Although the ancestral rite follows the same pattern of rites for the living, it is somewhat different because of the spiritual power associated with the dead soul. Many less-speculative Korean people tend to believe that the ancestral spirits are powerful enough to bestow blessings as well as to cause misfortune to the surviving members of the family. By observing ancestor worship regularly, the living believe themselves to be protected from disasters and showered with blessings. On the other hand, dead souls, if neglected, can cause trouble for the living family. In this respect, fear of the dead soul plays an important role in ancestor worship. This is hardly an expression of filial piety, however. When the rite comes to be associated with fear and with powers beyond the natural, it takes on the form of a religious act. Within this context ancestor worship becomes religious and takes the form of idolatry in the eyes of Christians.

What we have attempted so far is to prove that ancestor worship is neither a pure expression of filial piety nor a pure expression of religious devotion; it has both elements. It is, therefore, unfair to conclude that ancestor worship is purely ethical and cultural and has nothing to do with idolatry. It is also unfair to say that it is pure idolatry, by dismissing its cultural and ethical dimensions. Those who want to make ancestor worship a purely moral and cultural act are as wrong as those who want to make it an act of pure idolatry. What is needed is to combine both of these facets together when we consider ancestor worship in Korea.

What, then, is a Christian response to the practice of ancestor worship? First of all, we must recognize the idolatrous character of ancestor worship, while at the same time admitting that it is a part of a cultural heritage that is a precious gift of God to the Korean people. If we do not take the cultural heritage seriously, we can simply renounce the practice of ancestor worship altogether as an act of idolatry. This was done, in fact, by the early Christians. However, it was clearly a mistake. When a person gives up his own culture, he is less than fully human. The culture has to be retained as a precious gift of God. Therefore, we cannot renounce ancestor worship, because we are Christians. What we need to do with the practice of ancestor worship is to retain it as a cultural and ethical heritage while at the same time nullifying its idolatrous character. How can we do this?

It will be helpful to consider for a moment what it is that makes a man to be a Christian. What makes him different from a non-Christian is not his culture, but his commitment to Christ. This commitment makes him worship only one God, who revealed Himself through Christ. In other words, a Christian can have a new perspective on life. Through this new perspective, the old tradition has to be renewed. A renewal of ancestor worship is then needed that projects all things from the perspective of the Christian faith. To put things into a Christian perspective means to put Christ above the ancestral spirits. If Christ is seen to be the Lord and Master of all ancestral spirits, then we need not fear the powers of the dead soul. But the idolatrous character of ancestor worship comes precisely from this power of the dead soul. By placing Christ above these powers, we are free from the fear of ancestral souls. We come under the power of Christ, just as the ancestral souls are also under his power. At the ancestor-worship ceremonies, the focus of our worship is no longer upon the ancestral spirits but upon the God who was revealed in Christ.

Ancestor worship then becomes a proper form of Christian worship in which dead souls participate in communion with the living. This idea is acceptable to a Christian tradition that extols the communion of the saints. The ancestral souls can be treated as saints who have died. If a Christian believes that he can have communion with dead saints, as most Catholics do, then we should have no problem in accepting our communion with the dead souls of our ancestors at the ancestor-worship service. How meaningful to have a service of worship in communion with our dead ancestors! The community of worship is extended beyond the living. If we consciously make ourselves aware of the presence of our dead ancestors in our service to God, our service can be much more inclusive and meaningful. I hope that Christians in Korea will accept this new perspective on their ancestor worship. For Christians, ancestor worship can best be expressed as worship with ancestors rather than worship of ancestors.

Christians should not discard the form of ancestor worship. It is a part of Korean culture and should be retained as much as possible. My suggestion is to retain all of the forms of the ritual as it has been practiced in the past. The only change that Christians should make is to put it into a Christian perspective. This means that the ancestral tablets should still be placed on the altar; but above should stand the Cross of Christ. Christ would then be occupying the center of the worship service. The forms of prostration and offering can be the same as before; but the liturgy should be changed to fit into the Christian perspective. Moreover, the head of the household should act as a priest in the service as is done in ancestor worship. The altar should always stand at the center of the home and be regarded as a sanctuary. In this way ancestor worship would be changed into family worship together with ancestors. Ancestor worship would then be transformed into Christ worship. The misguided policy of eliminating the old and replacing it completely by the new can lead, in a way, to a denial of the gift of God to the Korean people. Better that Christ should transform the culture rather than replace it. Ancestor worship would then be transformed into a Christian family worship that includes not only the living members of the family but also its dead members as well.

Some Christians may ask the questions: "How can a Christian believe in the presence of dead souls in this world? Don't they go either to heaven or to hell when they die? Didn't Jesus say on the cross to the thief next to him that today he should be with him in paradise?" These questions seem to undermine the traditional belief of the Korean people in the presence of dead souls in <u>this</u> world. It is a mistake to believe, however, that hell or heaven or paradise are places somewhere far removed from this world. The location of hell or heaven should not be defined in terms of geography. It is to be understood in terms of religiousness, the relationship of oneself with God. To be in hell means to be removed from the presence of God; and to be in heaven means to be in communion with God. In this respect, the dead spirits or souls do not occupy any definite place or location. Rather, they are present without the limitation of any actual geographical boundaries.

That dead souls can exist without their physical bodies is not contrary to the Christian faith. As we have indicated before, the idea of saints occupies an important place in our Christian tradition. It is not only a Catholic belief but also a Protestant affirmation that we are in communion with the saints. We sing the hymn, "For all the saints who from labors rest..." Also, an "All Saints' Day" is observed by the more liturgical churches. It is, therefore, acceptable for Christians to think of the souls of their dead ancestors as saints. It is an expression of filial piety to treat our dead ancestors as saints. Just as Christians value their communion with the saints, so also Koreans esteem the communion with their dead ancestors. Korean Christians can then have communion not only with the Christian saints who died but also with their ancestral souls. To me it is a strength of Korean Christianity to include the souls of ancestors in their worship service. The Church is then conceived as the community of those living and dead who are brought together in Christ. In this way the Church transcends this world and reaches to the spiritual world.

I want to conclude with a personal note. One of my most pleasant memories from early childhood in Korea was that of the day of <u>Ch'u-sok</u>, when the Korean families visit their ancestral tombs. It was a beautiful autumn day when our family took food and wine and placed them before our ancestral tomb. We bowed down before it as children bowed down before their parents on New Year's day. My father then read a few verses from the Confucian liturgy. After the service was over and while we were sharing the food together, my father told us stories about our grandfather. It was a most meaningful experience for me to know my ancestor and to experience his presence with us. During that time I felt that the spirit of my grandfather was with us. It was an experience of true communion with my dead ancestor.

We should not abandon ancestor worship; it is a beautiful tradition that God has given us. We must transform this lovely tradition to reflect a Christian perspective. We should provide a Christian liturgy, instead of a Confucian one, in terms of which Christians can make ancestor worship into a Christian family worship together with ancestral souls. By so doing, the Christians in Korea have the opportunity to create a unique form of worship service that includes both the living and the dead.

STUDIES IN ASIAN THOUGHT AND RELIGION